Microsoft®

Outlook and Windows are registered trademarks of Microsoft Corporation.
All other trademarks quoted are the property of their respective editors.

All rights reserved. No part of this publication may be reproduced, stored in a retrieval system, or transmitted, in any form, or by any means, electronic, mechanical, photocopying, recording or otherwise, without the prior permission of the publishers.

Copyright - Editions ENI - May 2000
ISBN: 2-7460-0792-4
Original edition: ISBN: 2-7460-0720-7

ENI Publishing LTD

500 Chiswick High Road
London W4 5RG

Tel: 020 8956 2320
Fax: 020 8956 2321

e-mail: publishing@ediENI.com
http://www.publishing-eni.com

Editions ENI

BP 32125
44021 NANTES Cedex 1

Tel: 33.2.51.80.15.15
Fax: 33.2.51.80.15.16

e-mail: editions@ediENI.com
http://www.editions-eni.com

Straight to the point collection directed by Corinne HERVO

Foreword

The aim of this book is to let you find rapidly how to perform any task in **Outlook 2000** (the version used for the examples is the one supplied with Microsoft Office 2000; the message server is Microsoft Exchange Server version 5.5).

Each procedure is described in detail and illustrated so that you can put it into action easily.

The final pages are given over to an **index** of the topics covered and an **appendix**, which give details of shortcut keys and the description of the toolbars.

The typographic conventions used in this book are as follows:

Type faces used for specific purposes:	
bold	indicates the option to take in a menu or dialog box.
italic	is used for notes and comments.
[Ctrl]	represents a key from the keyboard; when two keys appear side by side, they should be pressed simultaneously.

Symbols indicating the content of a paragraph:	
▨	an action to carry out (activating an option, clicking with the mouse...).
⇨	a general comment on the command in question.
🖱	a technique which involves the mouse.
⌨	a keyboard technique.
📋	a technique which uses options from the menus.

OVERVIEW

1.1 The Outlook Environment 1
1.2 The interface 2

MESSAGES

2.1 Sending/editing messages 6
2.2 Receiving messages 14
2.3 Message contents 18
2.4 Mail configuration 25

CALENDAR

3.1 Calendar overview 32
3.2 Different Calendar items 36
3.3 Meetings 42
3.4 Printing a Calendar 47
3.5 Configuring the Calendar 49

OTHER FOLDERS

4.1 Outlook Today 50
4.2 The Contacts folder 52
4.3 The Tasks folder 60
4.4 The Notes folder 65
4.5 The Journal folder 68
4.6 Favorites Folder 70

Microsoft Outlook 2000

📖 ITEMS

    5.1   Managing items 72
    5.2   Categories of items 81
    5.3   Archiving items 82

📖 CUSTOMISING

    6.1   Views 86
    6.2   Groups and shortcuts 92
    6.3   Folders 94

APPENDIX

    Shortcut keys 99
    Toolbars 101
    Symbols 104

INDEX

    Index by subject 106

Microsoft Outlook 2000

1.1 The Outlook Environment

Microsoft Outlook is designed to enable you to manage private and professional data such as e-mail messages, meetings, business contacts, etc... You can also share information with other people through e-mail and even connect to the Internet.

A-Starting/leaving Outlook

- Click the **Start** button on the Windows desktop.
- Point to the **Programs** option and click **Microsoft Outlook**.
- If necessary, choose the profile you want to use.

⇨ You can choose a profile if the *Prompt for a profile to be used* option is active in the *Options* dialog box *(Tools - Options - Mail Services* tab).

⇨ If a shortcut icon already appears on the Windows desktop, you can double-click it to start Outlook.

- To leave Outlook use:

  File   Click ⊠ in   Alt F4
  Exit   the Outlook window

B-Using the menus

- When you open a menu, the standard options are shown by default. As you work, the menu options adapt to show the most recently used commands.
  To see all the commands, click ⌄ or wait for 5 seconds and the full menu will appear automatically.

- To see the shortcut menu for an item, right-click the item. To remove the shortcut menu, click elsewhere or press Esc.

  A shortcut menu is a shortened menu that contains only commands for the selected item (toolbar, shortcut, etc...).

1.2 The interface

A-The workspace

The screen which first appears when you start Outlook may be slightly different from the one illustrated below:

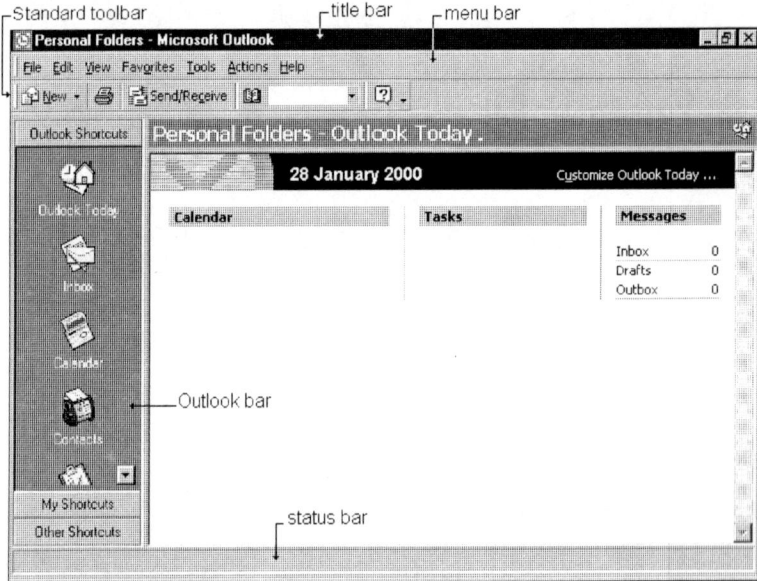

⇨ The status bar can be hidden or displayed using the **View - Status Bar** command, the Standard toolbar can be hidden or displayed using **View - Toolbars - Standard**. Two more toolbars can be shown using **View - Toolbars**: the **Advanced** and **Web** toolbars.

The Outlook bar

The Outlook bar gives you access to different groups; **Outlook Shortcuts, My Shortcuts,** and **Other Shortcuts**.

▪ To view the contents of one of the groups, click its name.

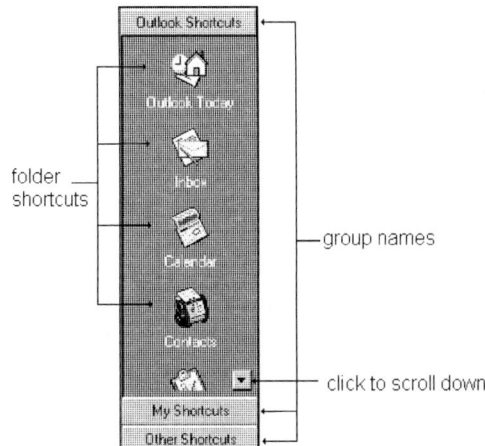

- The **Outlook Shortcuts** group contains the following folders:

Outlook Today	contains a whole day at a glance, including new messages and a list of tasks.
Inbox	contains messages which you have sent or received.
Calendar	contains all your appointments, events, pre-arranged meetings.
Contacts	contains a list of names and addresses of your business colleagues.
Tasks	contains all the tasks you have to do.
Notes	contains a list of notes which you have written either for yourself or others.
Deleted Items	contains all the items you have deleted from the other folders.

- The **My Shortcuts** group contains these folders:

Drafts	contains unfinished messages.
Outbox	contains the messages which need to be sent.
Sent Items	stores the messages you have sent.
Journal	contains journal entries like messages, notes, Microsoft Office documents.
Outlook Update	contains the Microsoft Office Web page for Outlook.

- The **Other Shortcuts** group contains folders which enable you to access your documents: **My Computer**, the **My documents** folder and the **Favorites** folder (which can display the most frequently used Web pages).

  ⇨ To show or hide the Outlook bar, use the *View - Outlook Bar* command. You can also right-click the bar then click *Hide Outlook Bar*.

  ⇨ Drag the right side of the bar to the right or the left to change its width.

  ⇨ When the *Outlook Today* folder is open, the *View - Go To* command enables you to go to the folders without using the Outlook bar.

Microsoft Outlook 2000

B-The Folder List

The **Folder List** displays Outlook folders in the form of a tree. It is particularly useful when the Outlook bar is hidden.

- To view the folder list temporarily, click the title of the folder which is currently active.

- Click the name of the folder whose contents you wish to see (as soon as you choose a folder, the list disappears and the name of the current folder changes).
- If you wish the folder list to remain on the screen use the command:

View
Folder List   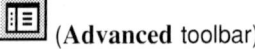 (**Adv**anced toolbar)

⇨ The same command can be used to hide the list.

C-Showing/hiding the preview pane

- Go to a folder other than **Outlook Today**.
- **View**
  Preview Pane  (**Advanced** toolbar)

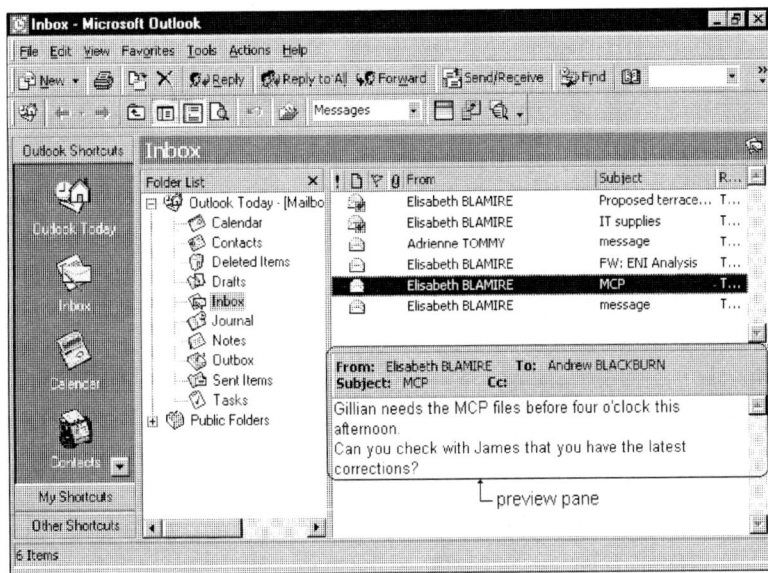

⇨ *Use the same command to hide the preview pane.*

Microsoft Outlook 2000

2.1 Sending/editing messages

Electronic mail is a means of sending and receiving messages electronically. Four folders can contain messages: Inbox (Outlook Shortcuts), Drafts, Outbox and Sent Items (My Shortcuts).

A-Creating a message

▪ File - New - Mail message or `Ctrl` `⇧ Shift` **M**
or
Go to a message folder and click the **New** button on the Standard toolbar or use **File - New - Mail Message** (`Ctrl` **N**) or **Actions - New - Mail Message**.

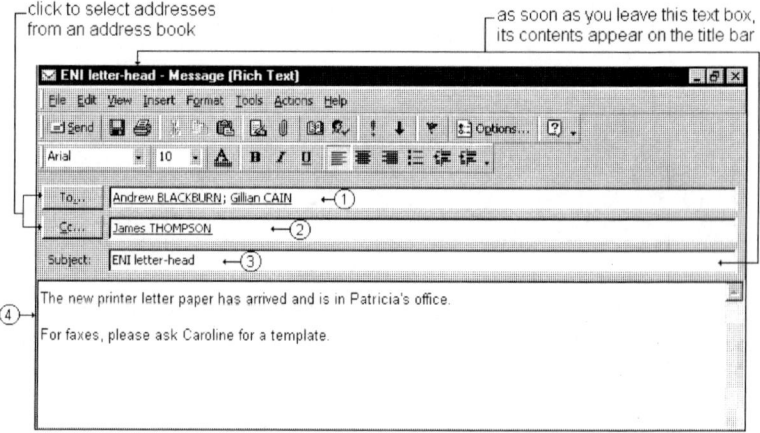

① Enter the name and address of the message recipient (if there are several recipients, enter their names separated by semi-colons).

② Enter the name and address of any recipients to whom you wish to send a copy of the message (and from whom you do not require a reply).

③ Enter the subject of the message.

④ Enter the text of the message.

▪ Send the message.

⇨ When you leave the **To** box, if Outlook recognises the recipient's address, it is underlined, providing the option **Automatic name checking** is active. To access this option, go to the main Outlook window and use **Tools - Options - Preferences** tab. Click the **E-mail Options** button then the **Advanced E-mail Options** button.

⇨ If you wish to send a message to other users but to keep their identity hidden, display the **Bcc** field (**View - Bcc Field**).

6

⇨ The addresses in the *To*, *Cc* and *Bcc* fields may have an Internet E-mail format (jsmith@eni.com).

⇨ You can create messages using Word as the editor or using a particular format (See 2.4 - A - Choosing the default message format).

⇨ You can create messages with other Office applications using the command *Actions - New Mail Message Using - Microsoft Office*: choose the type of message you want to create: *Microsoft Word Document, Microsoft PowerPoint Slide, Microsoft Excel Worksheet* or *Microsoft Access Data Page*.

B-Creating a message on stationery

Actions - New Mail Message Using - More Stationery

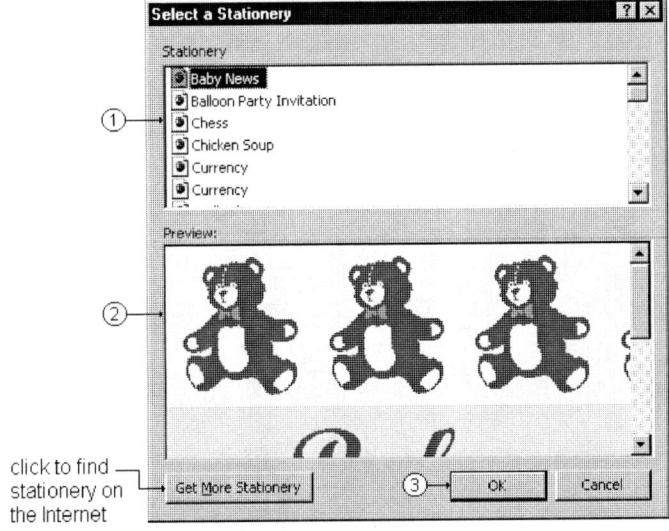

click to find stationery on the Internet

① Choose your stationery.
② Preview it.
③ Confirm your choice.

Continue as you would with any message.

⇨ After you have used stationery, its name appears in the *Actions - New Mail Message Using* menu. Simply click it to create a new message with the same stationery.

⇨ If you choose to create a message using stationery, the message format will automatically be HTML.

C-Sending a Web page in a message

- Use the Web toolbar to open the Web page concerned.
- Actions - Send Web Page by E-Mail

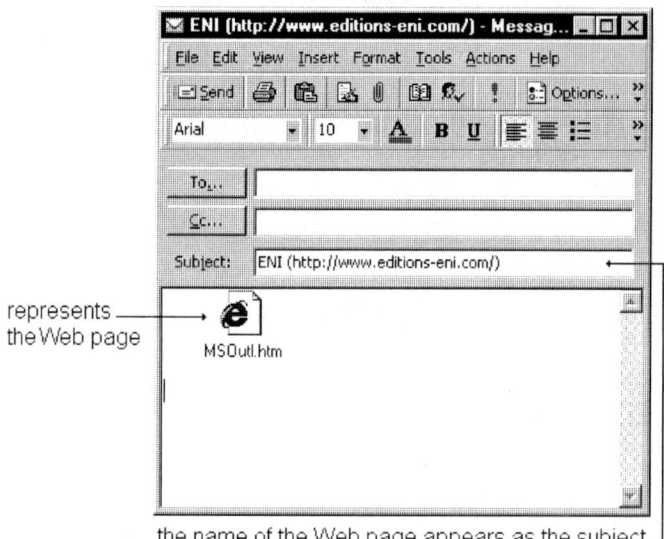

represents the Web page

the name of the Web page appears as the subject

- Continue the message (choosing recipients, change the subject...) and send it.

D-Saving and closing an unfinished message

- File   Save   Ctrl S

- Close your message:
  File   Click the ✗ button in   Alt F4
  Close   the message window

The message is stored in the **Drafts** folder in the **My Shortcuts** group and is preceded by the symbol.

⇨ To edit a message, click the **Drafts** folder in the **My Shortcuts** group and double-click the message.

⇨ By default, messages that you are creating are saved in the **Drafts** folder every 3 minutes. To deactivate this feature, use **Tools - Options - Preferences** tab. Click the **E-mail Options** button and deactivate **Automatically save unsent messages**. To change the frequency of the saves, click **Advanced E-mail options** in the **E-mail Options** dialog box.

⇨ You can close a message without saving it.

E- Sending a message

- Once you have created or modified a message, use:
  File
  Send
  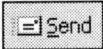

⇨ After a message has been sent, it is stored in the sender's **Sent Items** folder. The recipient finds the message stored in his **Inbox**, preceded by the ✉ symbol for unread messages. If sending the message has not been possible it is stored in the **Outbox** folder.

⇨ If you do not want to keep all your sent items you can deactivate the option **Save copies of messages in Sent Items Folder** in the **E-mail Options** dialog box (Tool - Options - Preferences tab, E-mail Options button).

F- Selecting recipients from an address book

- When you are creating or modifying a message click the **To** and **Cc** buttons to select the recipient from an address book.

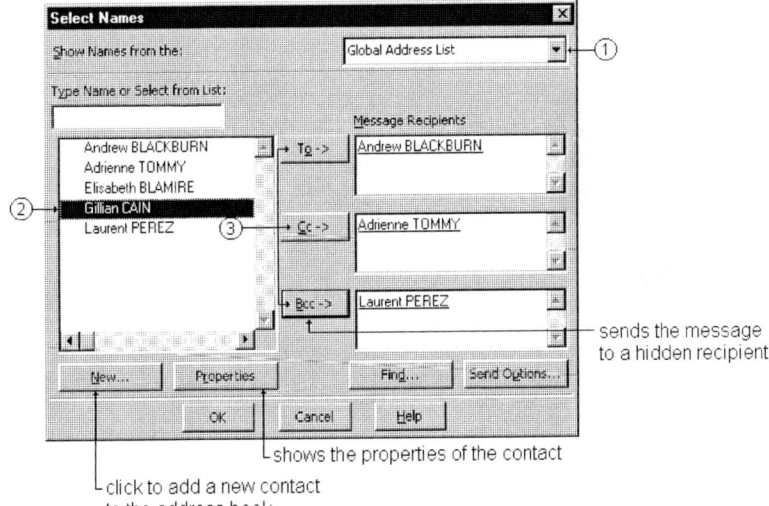

① Select the address book.

② Select the recipient's name.

③ Click the appropriate button.

- To remove a name, click the name in the **Message Recipients** box and press the Del key.
- Click **OK** and continue creating or modifying your message.

Microsoft Outlook 2000

G-Selecting recipients before creating a message

- Open the **Outlook Shortcuts** group in the **Outlook** bar and click the **Contacts** icon.
- Select the different message recipients.
- Actions
  New Message to Contact

⇨ *In the message window which appears, the To field is already filled in.*

H-Sending the same message again

- Open the **Sent Items** folder in the **My Shortcuts** group and double-click the message that you want to send again.
- Actions - Resend This Message
- Modify the message, if you need to, then send it.

I- Recalling/replacing a message already sent

It is possible to recall or replace a message that has already been sent, providing that it has not yet been read by its recipients. This feature is only available with Microsoft Exchange Server.

- Open your **Sent Items** folder in the **My Shortcuts** group.
- Double-click the message to be recalled or replaced.
- Actions - Recall This Message

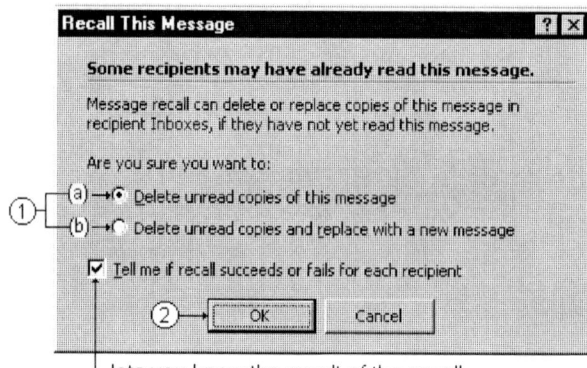

lets you know the result of the recall

① Choose:
  (a) to recall the message.
  (b) to replace the message.
② Confirm.

- If you decided to replace the message, modify it then send it and close the message window.

J- Flagging a message

A flag is used to mark a message that requires a particular follow up. Depending on the flag you choose, a comment reminding you of the necessary follow up actions appears at the top of the message.

Inserting a message flag

- When you are creating or modifying a message, go into:
  Actions   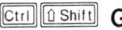 G
  Flag for Follow Up

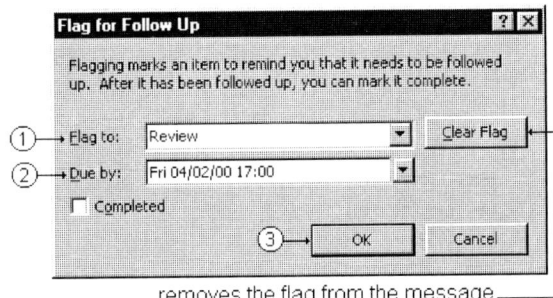

removes the flag from the message

① Choose a flag text.
② If necessary, give a due date.
③ Confirm.

⇒ Messages containing a flag appear with this symbol .

⇒ The view *By Follow Up Flag* filters messages by flag. If you want to limit the list to messages whose due date falls within the next seven days choose the *Flagged for Next Seven Days* view.

⇒ You can flag messages you have received.

Indicating that the follow-up has been completed

- Select the message that has been followed up.
- Actions  G
  Flag for Follow Up
- Activate the **Completed** option and enter.

⇒ *Messages which are completed are shown with the* ☑ *symbol.*

Microsoft Outlook 2000

K-Giving a message an importance rating

▪ While you are creating or modifying your message, click the Options... button.

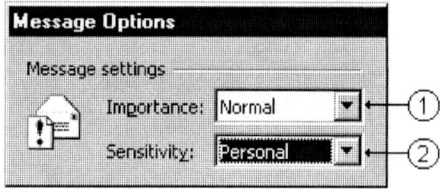

① Indicate the importance rating of your message: **Low**, **Normal** or **High**.

② Define the nature of the message:

Normal	Indicates that it is a standard message.
Personal	Indicates that the message contents are of a personal nature.
Private	Protects the message from being modified after it has been sent.
Confidential	Indicates that access to the message is restricted to a certain number of people, or is of a private nature.

▪ Click **Close** and continue your message.

⇨ Messages of high priority are preceded by this symbol, and those of low priority with this one. The sensitivity criteria, however, are only displayed when the message is opened. A reminder of the message's priority is also displayed when the message is opened.

⇨ You can also indicate the importance of a message while you are creating it by using the High and Low importance buttons.

⇨ By default, every new message is given normal importance and sensitivity ratings. To modify this, go into **Tools - Options**, then, on the **Preferences** tab, click the **E-mail Options** button. Next, click **Advanced E-mail Options** to choose your default options in the **Set importance** and **Set sensitivity** lists.

⇨ It is also possible to filter information according to the importance of the items. On the **More Choices** page in the **Actions - Find All - Related Messages** dialog box, activate the **Whose importance is** option then choose **normal**, **high** or **low**.

L- Sending a message whose reply involves voting

This option is only available if you are working with Microsoft Exchange Server.

- While you are creating the message, click **Options...**.

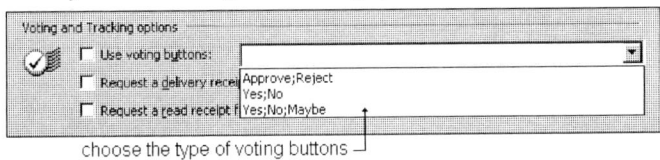

choose the type of voting buttons you want to insert

You can create your own voting options, using a semi-colon to separate them.

⇨ *These voting buttons appear when the recipient reads the message. They allow him or her to reply to the message and cast their vote.*

⇨ *Once the recipients have voted, the replies appear in the sender's Inbox. You can also read them by opening the voting message and activating the* **Tracking** *tab.*

M-Sending a message with tracking options

- When you create a message, click **Options...**.
- In the **Voting and Tracking options** frame, activate the **Request a delivery receipt for this message** option if you want to receive a message telling you the date and time the message arrived in the recipient's Inbox.
- Activate **Request a read receipt for this message** if you want to receive a message telling you the date and time at which the recipient opened the message.
- Click the **Close** button and continue your message.

When you open a message in which you have activated one or both of the tracking options, there is a second tab in the window, (the **Tracking** *tab). The system will take a moment before displaying this tab.*

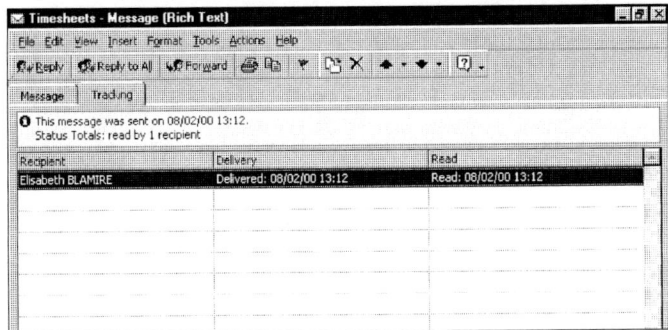

Microsoft Outlook 2000

N-Defining delivery options

- While you are creating your message click the 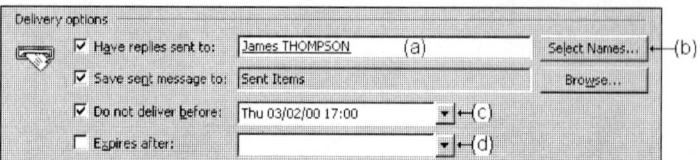 button.

- If you want to delegate the reception or replies to another user, enter their name in (a) or use button (b).
- To delay the sending of a message, open the list (c) and enter the appropriate date and time.
- To cancel a message that has not been sent by a certain date, open the list (d) and give the date.
- Click **Close** and continue your message.

2.2 Receiving messages

A-Reading a message you have received

- Open your Inbox.

  Unread messages are presented in bold type with the following symbol:

- Show the preview pane if you want to then click in the message you want to read, or double-click the message.

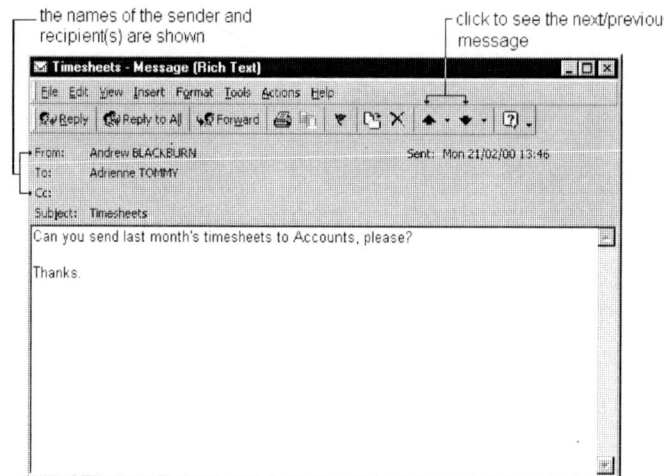

⇨ As soon as you consult a message it is regarded as read: these messages are preceded by this symbol: ◻.

⇨ To find unread messages more easily, select the **Unread Message** view. Of course, as soon as a message is opened and subsequently closed, it disappears from the list!

B-Marking messages as read or unread

▪ Select the messages to be marked.
▪ **Edit - Mark as Read** or **Mark as Unread** or [Ctrl] Q

⇨ Choose the **Edit - Mark All as Read** command to mark all the items in a folder as read.

⇨ To find messages which have been read, activate the **Only items that are** option then select **read** in the **Advanced Find** dialog box (**Actions - Find All - Related Messages - More Choices**).

C-Replying to a message

▪ Open the message you want to reply to or select it without opening it.
▪ To reply to the message sender, use:

Actions      [Ctrl] R
Reply

To reply to the sender and to the other recipients as well, use:

Actions      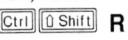 R
Reply to All

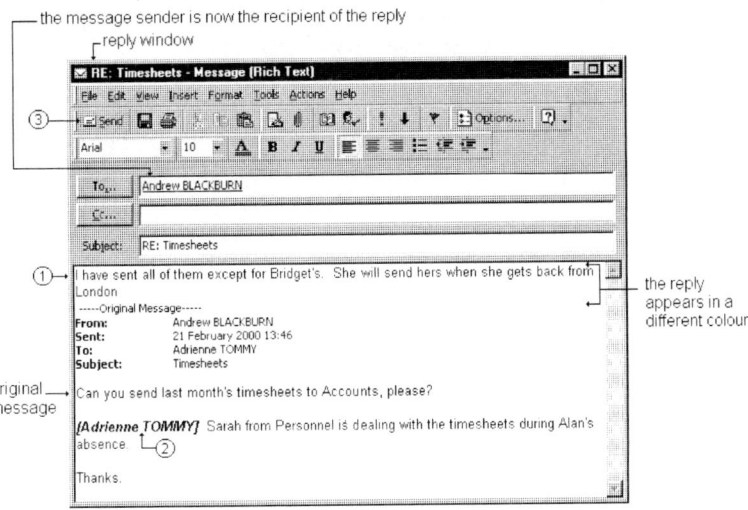

Microsoft Outlook 2000 — 15

① Enter your reply at the top of the text field.

② If you wish to, make changes to the original message. The text you have entered or modified will now appear in blue. Your name will also appear in blue and within brackets, provided that the **Mark my comments with** option is active in the **E-mail Options** dialog box (**Tools - Options - Preferences** tab - **E-mail Options** button).

③ Send your reply.

⇨ *The date and time of your reply appear in the original message window.*

⇨ *In the sender's **Inbox** the message is marked ; in his/her **Sent Items** folder the message subject is now preceded by the indication **RE**.*

⇨ *To avoid going back into the original message once you have sent a reply, activate the option **Close original message on reply or forward** in the **Advanced E-mail Options** dialog box (**Tools - Options - Preferences** tab - **E-mail Options** button then **Advanced E-mail Options** button).*

⇨ *To change the appearance of your replies, go to the **E-mail Options** dialog box and choose an option from the **When replying to a message** list.*

D-Forwarding a message

You can forward a message to a user who was not one of the original recipients.

▪ Select or open the message.

▪ **Actions** 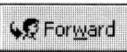 Ctrl F
  Forward

The subject of the message has been retained but now it is preceded by the indication **FW**. In the text field, Outlook reminds you of the **Original Message**.

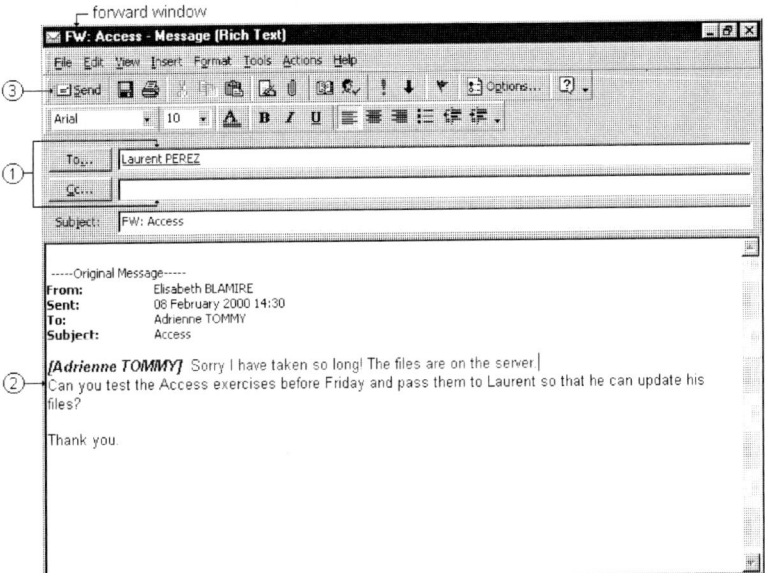

① Enter the names of the new recipients.

② If necessary, add your comments, (which are in blue, possibly preceded by your name between square brackets).

③ Send the message.

- Close the message you are currently reading.

⇨ In the sender's **Inbox**, forwarded messages are marked with the symbol while in his/her **Sent Items** folder the subject of the message is preceded by the indication **FW**.

⇨ To avoid going back into the original message once it has been forwarded, activate the option **Close original message on reply or forward** in the **E-mail Options** dialog box (**Tools - Options - Preferences** tab - **E-mail Options** button).

⇨ To change the appearance of your forwarded messages, go to the **E-mail Options** dialog box and choose an option from the **When forwarding a message** list.

⇨ To avoid saving duplicate copies of forwarded messages, deactivate the **Save forwarded messages** option in the **Advanced E-mail Options** dialog box (**Tools - Options - Preferences** tab - **E-mail Options** button then **Advanced E-mail Options** button). This ensures that forwarded messages are only stored in the **Inbox**.

Microsoft Outlook 2000

E-Voting in reply to a message

- Open the message.

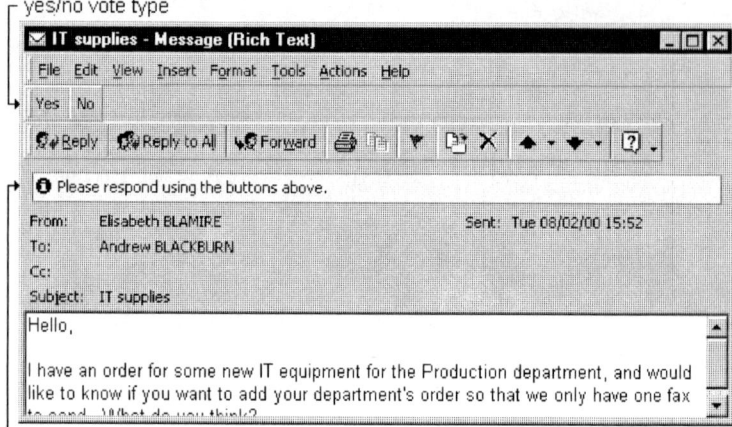

- Click the button that corresponds to your choice.
- Decide whether or not to edit the response and add a comment then close the original message.

2.3 Message contents

A-Checking spelling in a message

The instructions below suppose that you are not using Microsoft Word as your default message editor (See 2.4 - A - Choosing the default message format). If Word is your message editor, you will be using its spelling checker.

- If you wish to check all the message text, position the pointer at the beginning of the text; if you only want to check one part of the text, select it.
- **Tools - Spelling** or F7

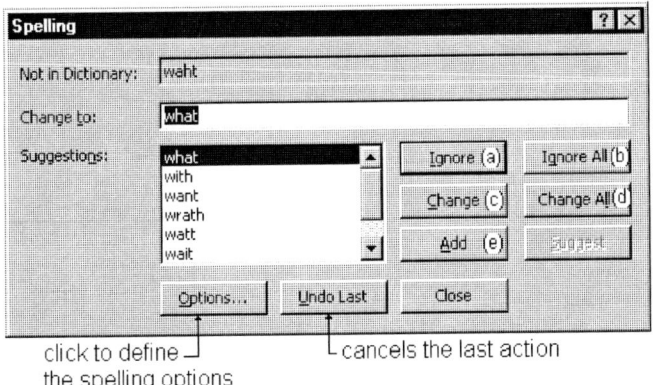

click to define ⌐ ⌐ cancels the last action
the spelling options

- Click one of the following buttons:
  - (a) leave the selected word unchanged and continue with the spelling-check.
  - (b) leave all occurrences of the word unchanged.
  - (c) replace the selected word in the **Not in Dictionary** field with that suggested in the **Change to** field.
  - (d) replace all occurrences of the word displayed in the **Not in Dictionary** field with that suggested in the **Change to** field.
  - (e) add the selected word to the dictionary.
- When Outlook tells you that the spelling check is complete, click **OK**.

B-Formatting text

- If you have already entered text, drag to select it.
- Use the buttons available on the **Formatting** toolbar.

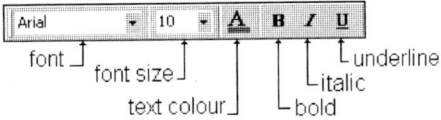

font ⌐ ⌐ underline
font size ⌐ ⌐ italic
text colour ⌐ ⌐ bold

⇨ If the **Formatting** toolbar is not visible, right-click one of the toolbars, then click **Formatting** to display it.

⇨ You can cancel all the formatting effects in one action using the [Ctrl] [space] shortcut key combination.

⇨ You can also use **Format - Font** to format text.

C-Formatting paragraphs

- Click inside the paragraph concerned or if there are more than one, select them.

Microsoft Outlook 2000

- Use the buttons on the **Formatting** toolbar:

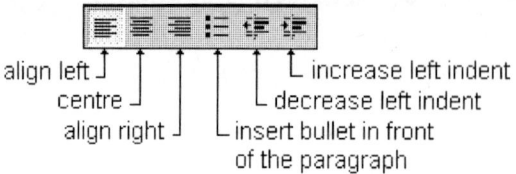

align left ⏐ ⏐ ⏐ ⏐ ⏐ increase left indent
centre ⏐ ⏐ ⏐ decrease left indent
align right ⏐ insert bullet in front
of the paragraph

⇨ You can also modify the alignment and add bullets from the **Format - Paragraph** menu.

D-Inserting a signature

To be able to use this feature, you need first to have created a signature.
- Place the insertion point where you want to insert the signature.
- **Insert Signature**
- Click the name of the signature you want to insert.

⇨ You can configure Outlook so that a signature is inserted into each new message automatically (see 2.4 - B - Creating signatures).

E-Attaching a document

- Position the insertion point where you want to insert the document.
- **Insert File**

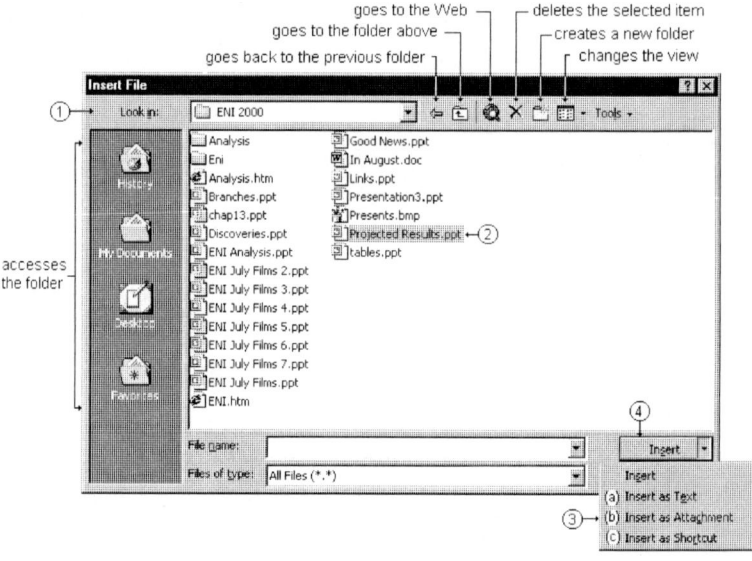

goes to the Web — deletes the selected item
goes to the folder above — creates a new folder
goes back to the previous folder — changes the view

① accesses the folder

② Projected Results.ppt

③ (a) Insert as Text
(b) Insert as Attachment
(c) Insert as Shortcut

④ Insert

20

① Select the drive where the file is located.
② Select the name of the document to be inserted in the message.
③ Indicate how the file should be inserted:
- (a) Inserts the document as text in the message body (the text cannot contain presentation items).
- (b) Inserts the document as an attachment (the document is copied to the **Temp folder** on your disk).
- (c) Inserts a shortcut to the document. Use this option for large files/folders.

④ Confirm.

▪ Send the message.

If you have chosen the (b) or (c) option, the selected document appears as an icon in the message. Double-click this icon to open the enclosed document.

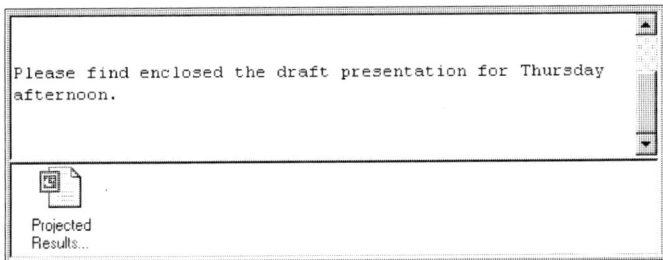

F-Inserting an Outlook item

▪ Place the insertion point where the item is to be inserted.
▪ Insert - Item

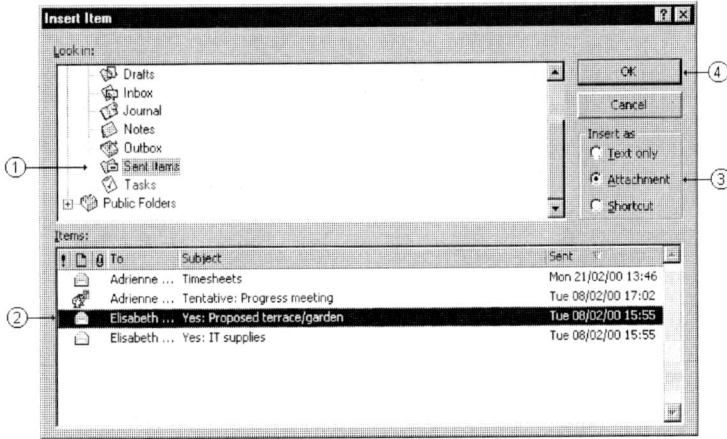

① Indicate in which folder the item can be found.

Microsoft Outlook 2000

② Select the item to be inserted (you can select more than one).
③ Choose how to insert the item. When you insert items as text or attachments, the data in the item is copied, unlike a shortcut insertion, which creates a hyperlink to the original item.
④ Confirm.

the inserted items appear as icons indicating their origin

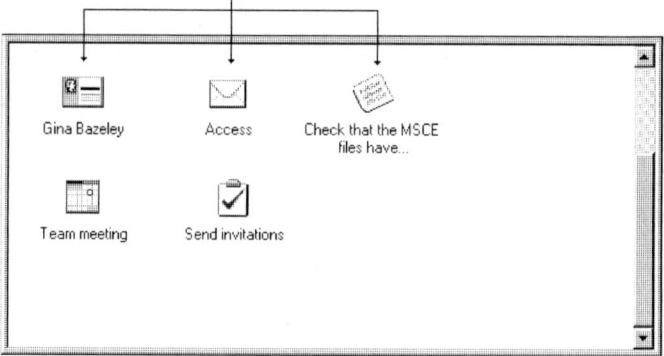

G-Inserting an object

You can insert an existing or new object by means of OLE (Object Linking and Embedding).

- Position the insertion point where you want to insert the object.
- **Insert - Object**

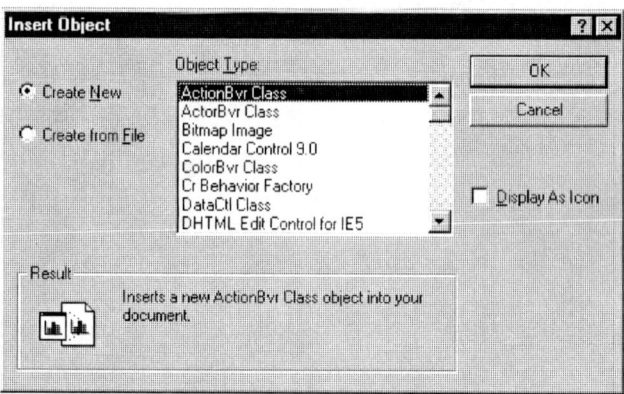

- Leave the **Create New** option active if you want to insert a new document, then select the type of object you want to create from the **Object Type** list. Click **OK**.

  The application you have chosen starts: its menus and toolbars temporarily replace those of Outlook.

- Create the object that you want to insert then click outside the object's frame to leave the application.

▪ To insert an existing object, activate the **Create from File** option then click the **Browse** button to select the document. Activate the **Link** option if you wish to establish a link with the object rather than embedding it.

⇨ Double-click the object to start its server application.

⇨ You cannot insert an object into a plain text or HTML format message.

H-Improving the look of an HTML message

Inserting a horizontal line

▪ Place the insertion point where you want to insert the line.
▪ **Insert - Horizontal Line**

Inserting a picture

▪ Place the insertion point where you want the picture to appear.
▪ **Insert - Picture**

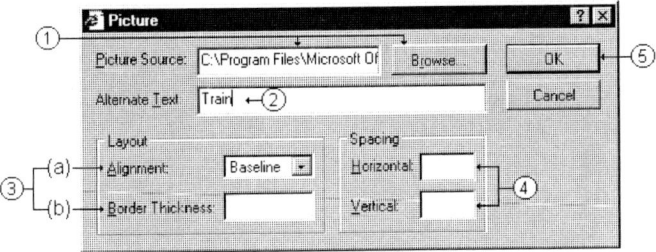

① Indicate the source of the picture.
② Enter a caption for the picture, if necessary.
③ Choose the formatting options:

    (a)   the alignment of the picture in relation to the baseline.
    (b)   add a border for which you need to indicate the thickness.

④ Choose the horizontal and/or vertical spacing of the picture in relation to the left and/or top margins.
⑤ Insert the picture.

Applying a background picture or colour

▪ To insert a background picture, use **Format - Background - Picture**, enter the name of the picture (or use the **Browse** button to find it) then confirm.

▪ Apply a background colour using **Format - Background - Color**, and click the colour you want.

⇨ You cannot have a background colour and picture at the same time.

⇨ To remove the picture, use **Format - Background - Picture**, select the picture's name and press [Del].

Microsoft Outlook 2000

I- Inserting a hyperlink

This operation allows you to send the address of a Web site in your message text. A hyperlink can only be inserted in an HTML format message.

▪ Place the insertion point where you want to insert the link or select the text that is to be the link.

▪ **Insert - Hyperlink**

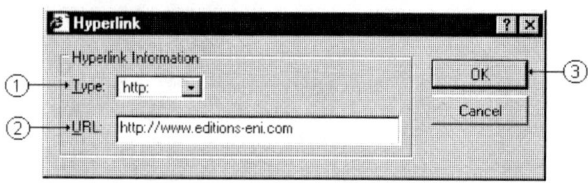

① Indicate the file type.
② Enter the URL address.
③ Confirm.

⇨ *When the recipient receives the message and clicks the link, they will go to the Web site in question.*

J- Printing messages

▪ To print just one message, select it or open it. To print several messages, select them from their folder.

▪ **File - Print** or Ctrl P

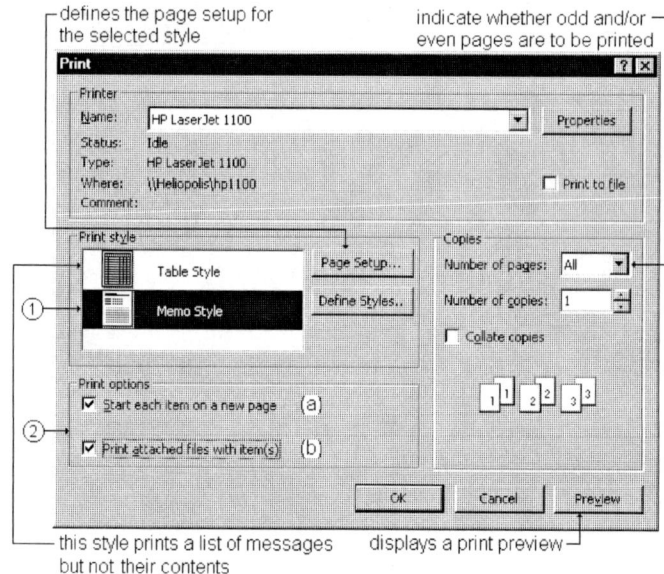

defines the page setup for the selected style

indicate whether odd and/or even pages are to be printed

this style prints a list of messages but not their contents

displays a print preview

① Select the memo print style.

② Define your printing options:

(a) if you have selected several messages, indicate whether you wish to start each one on a new page.

(b) if the items have attachments, activate this option so that each attached file is also printed.

- Click **OK** to start printing.

⇨ With the 🖨 button you can start printing right away using the parameters which are currently active.

⇨ Click the 🔍 button to obtain a print preview.

2.4 Mail configuration

A - Choosing the default message format

- **Tools - Options**
- Activate the **Mail Format** tab.

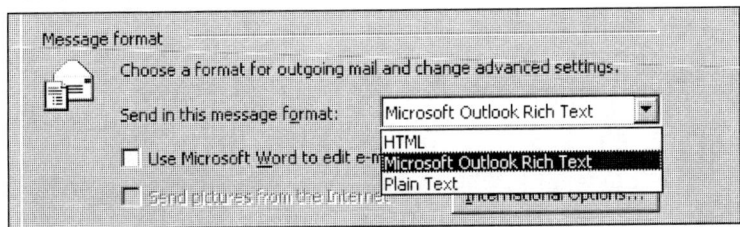

- Choose the type of format you want to use by default in the **Send in this message format** list:

Plain Text — your messages cannot contain any formatting, but they will be completely legible to all recipients who receive them over the Internet.

Microsoft Outlook Rich Text — you can apply formatting (to characters, paragraphs) but if your messages are sent over the Internet the recipients will not receive the formatting. This format is also called RTF.

HTML — you can apply a large amount of formatting (background, hyperlinks, stationery...). Note that HTML messages have a longer download time.

- Activate the **Use Microsoft Word to edit e-mail messages** option if you want Word to be your message editor.

Microsoft Outlook 2000

⇨ Whichever default format you choose, you can always create a new message based on a different format by using **Actions - New Mail Message Using**.

⇨ If Microsoft Word is not your default message editor, you can still use it as such with the command **Actions - New Mail Message Using - Microsoft Word (Rich Text)**.

B-Creating signatures

- **Tools - Options - Mail Format** tab
- Click the **Signature Picker** button then **New**.
- Enter the name you want to give the signature.
- Indicate how you want to create your signature: **Start with a blank signature**, **Use this existing signature as a template** (choose the existing signature you want to use) or **Use this file as a template** (choose the file you want to use).
- Click **Next**.

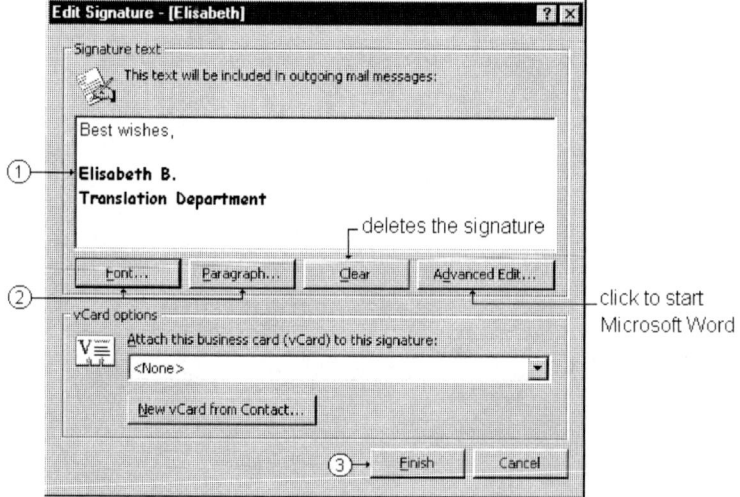

① Type the signature text.
② Format the text.
③ Confirm.

- Create all the signatures you require in this way then close the **Signature Picker** dialog box by clicking **OK**.

⇨ To insert a signature automatically, use **Tools - Options**. Activate the **Mail Format** tab and select your default signature in the **Use this signature by default** list.

C-Configuring Outlook to alert you when you receive a new message

- Tools - Options
- Click the **E-mail Options** button on the **Preferences** tab.
- Activate the **Display a notification message when new mail arrives** option.

This window appears whenever a new message arrives:

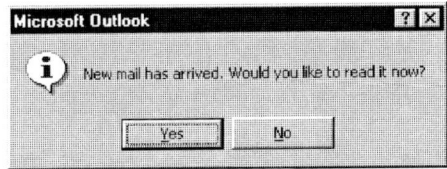

⇨ By default, only a sound and a momentary change in the shape of the mouse pointer indicate the arrival of a new message.

D-Managing your e-mail during your absence

This feature is only available to users working on Microsoft Exchange Server.

Signalling your absence

You can configure Outlook to send a message automatically to any user who tries to contact you during your absence.

- In the main Outlook window, use **Tools - Out of Office Assistant**
- Activate the **I am currently Out of the Office** option.
- Enter the text of the message that will be sent during your absence (this message will only be sent once to each user) and confirm.

⇨ When you return, activate the **I am currently In the Office** option in the **Out of Office Assistant** dialog box. This will not delete the messages sent to users during your absence.

Managing messages during your absence

- Activate one of the message folders in the main window.
- **Tools - Out of Office Assistant**
- Click the **Add Rule** button.

Microsoft Outlook 2000

① Define the conditions of the rule you are creating.
② Define what Outlook should do.
③ Confirm.

The new rule is added to the existing ones.

Managing the out of office rules

- Tools - Out of Office Assistant

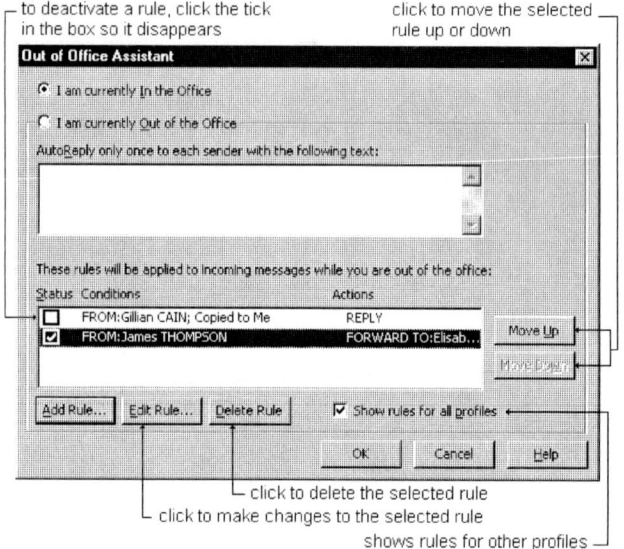

28

E- Organising messages from a contact

- Activate the folder that contains the messages you want to organise.
- Tools
  Organize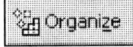

Moving messages from a particular contact

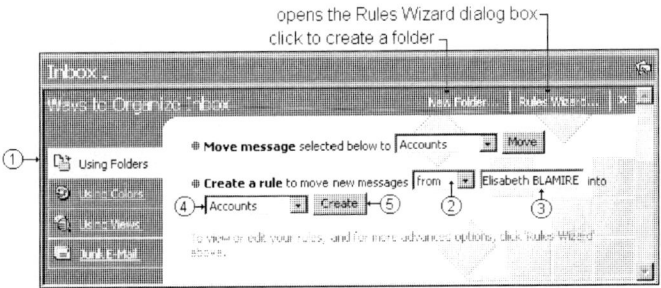

① Activate this tab.

② Choose the type of messages: **from** or **sent to**.

③ Enter the name of the contact whose messages are going to be moved (you can click a message concerning them).

④ Enter the name of the folder to which the messages are to be sent; if this folder does not exist, create it using the **New Folder** button.

⑤ Create the rule.

In this example, all new messages from **Elisabeth BLAMIRE** *will be moved from the* **Inbox** *to the* **Accounts** *folder.*

⇨ *By using the* **Organize** *window, you can move selected messages (not necessarily from a given contact) to a given folder (see 5.1 - G - Moving items to another folder).*

Applying a colour to messages from a particular contact

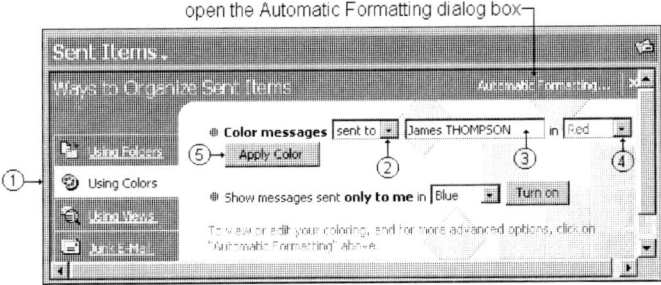

① Click this tab.

② Choose the message type: **from** or **sent to**.

③ Indicate the contact concerned.

Microsoft Outlook 2000 29

④ Choose the colour you want to use.
⑤ Create the rule.

⇨ *You can also choose a colour for messages that have been sent only to you by using the* **Show messages sent only to me in** *colour list.*

Managing unwanted mail

Outlook can filter messages according to their contents and/or their origin. The list of filter options is in a file called Filters.txt.

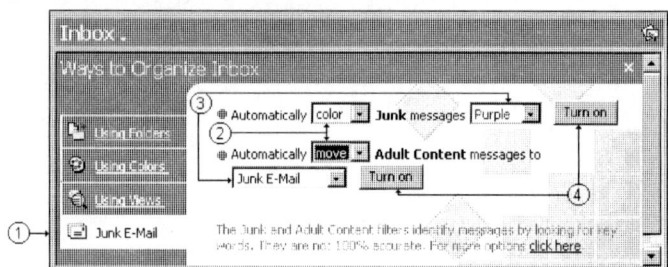

① Activate this tab.
② Choose what to do: **color** or **move**.
③ Choose the colour and/or the destination folder.
④ Confirm the rule(s).

F-Managing messages using the Rules Wizard

▪ Activate the folder containing the messages to be filed.
▪ **Tools**
  Rules Wizard
▪ Click the **New** button.

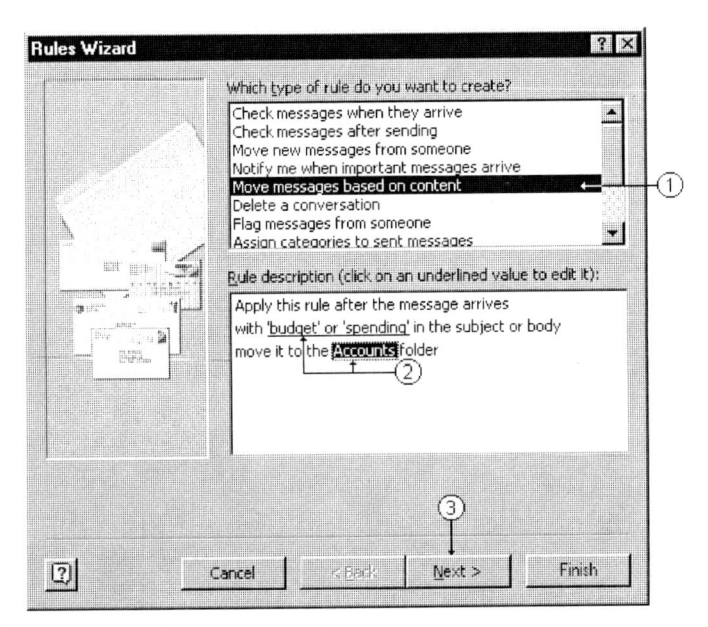

① Select the type of rule you want to create.
② Define the rule.
③ Go to the next step.

3.1 Calendar overview

The *Calendar* is a tool that allows you to organise your schedule and make best possible use of your time. It can manage three activities (or items): appointments, meetings and events.

A-Viewing the Calendar

Click the **Outlook Shortcuts** group in the Outlook bar, then click the **Calendar** shortcut. If the Outlook bar is hidden, open the folder list and click **Calendar**.

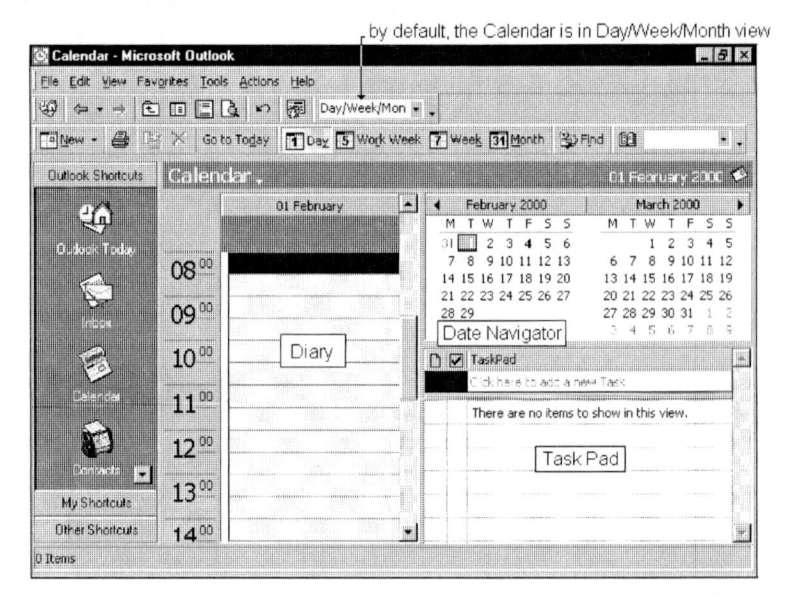

by default, the Calendar is in Day/Week/Month view

B-Different Calendar views

In **Day/Week/Month** view there are four different time-scales.

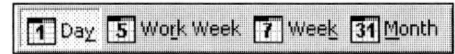

⇨ You can also use the *View - Day* or *WorkWeek* or *Week* or *Month* commands.

Viewing a month

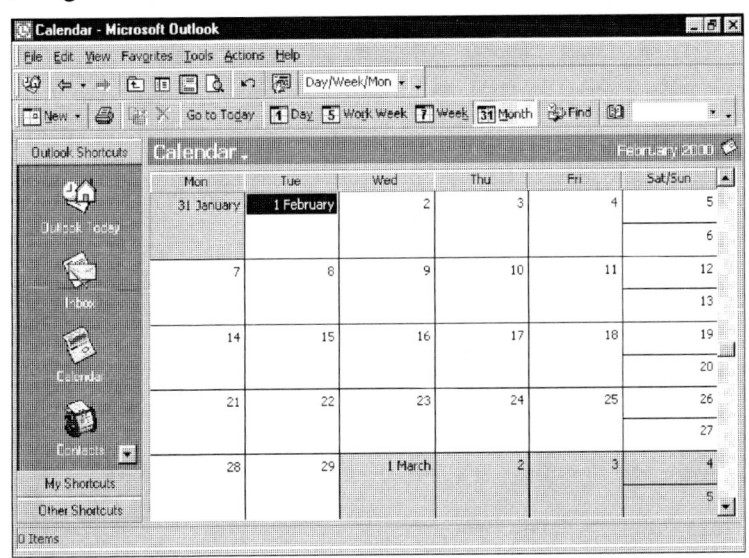

Only the Diary pane is visible. Alternate months appear with grey backgrounds. In this style of presentation the weekends are compressed.

⇨ To give Saturdays and Sundays the same space as the weekdays use the **View - Current View - Customize Current View** command. Click the **Other Settings** button, deactivate the **Compress weekend days** option and click **OK** twice.

⇨ In this view you can reach the first day of the month by pressing [Alt] [Pg Up], and the last by pressing [Alt] [Pg Dn].

Microsoft Outlook 2000

Viewing a week

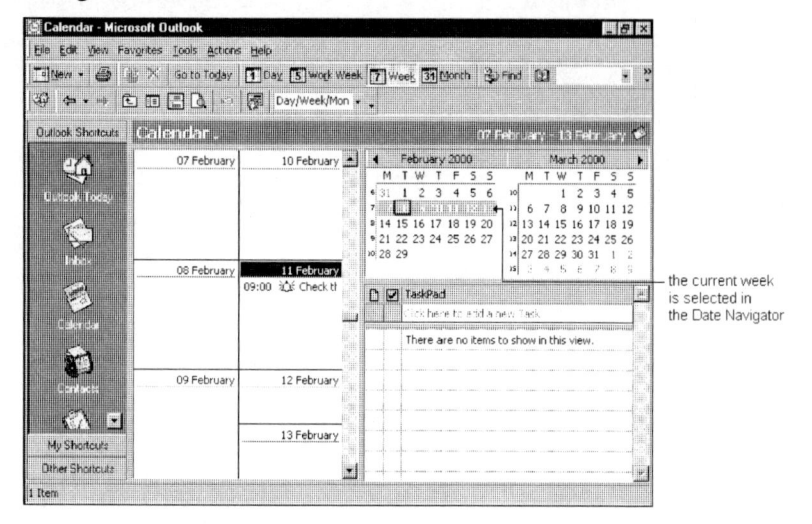

⇨ Define the display options for appointment times using the command: **View - Current View - Customize Current View - Other Settings** button. Define the view options for appointments (for weeks and months) using *Show time as clocks* and *Show end time*.

Viewing one or more days at a time

- To define how many days to view, and which ones, select the days required in the Date Navigator pane, holding down the [Ctrl] key to select non-consecutive dates.

- Use the following key combinations to change the number of days being displayed.

    View 1 to 9 days   [Alt] + n where n is the number of consecutive days to display
    View 10 days   [Alt] 0
    View the week   [Alt] -
    View the month   [Alt] =

- To modify the time scale, use the **View - Current View - Customize Current View** command then click the **Other Settings** button, and choose the **Time scale**.

⇨ To change the fonts used in the Calendar click the **Font** button in the appropriate frame *(Day, Week or Month)*.

C-Changing the date

🖱 Use the Date Navigator:

previous month — scroll through the months by dragging the pointer up or down the list — next month

▦ View - Go To - Go to Date or `Ctrl` G

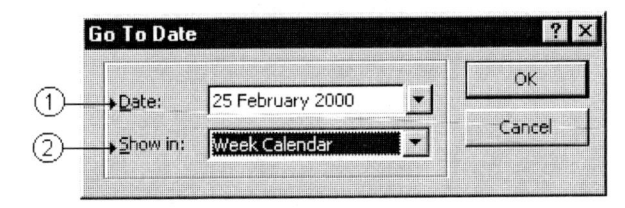

① Type in the date you want to reach.

② Indicate whether you want the **Day Calendar, Week Calendar** or **Month Calendar**.

⇨ To return to today's date use the **View - Go To - Go to Today** command or the `Go to Today` button.

D-Saving a calendar as a Web page

This technique allows you to publish a calendar on your company's intranet or your Internet site in order to share it with other users.

- In the **Outlook Shortcuts** group, click the **Calendar** folder.
- **File - Save as Web Page**

Microsoft Outlook 2000

① Indicate the start and end dates of the calendar.
② Use the **Browse** button to select a graphic to display in the background, if this is necessary.
③ Enter the calendar title (the user's name appears by default).
④ Give the file name (folder name or URL address).
⑤ Confirm the publication.

3.2 Different Calendar items

A- Creating an appointment

*An **appointment** is any activity for which you need to reserve time in your calendar but which does not necessarily involve other people.*

■ File - New - Appointment or [Ctrl][D Shift] **A**
or
open the **Calendar** folder and click the **New** button or use **Actions - New Appointment** ([Ctrl] **N**).

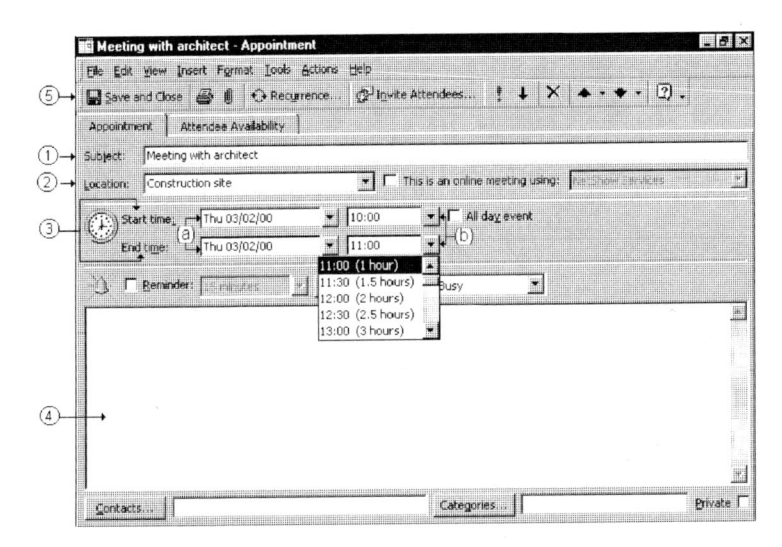

① Enter a description of the appointment.

② Either type in the location or select it from the list.

③ Enter the date of the appointment in (a) then define the start and end times in (b) (you can also enter your own time).

④ If necessary, add any extra details.

⑤ Save the appointment.

⇨ If you double-click a time-slot in the Diary pane, the **Appointment** window opens, enabling you to modify an existing appointment or create a new one.

⇨ By default, appointments last half an hour. To help you define the **End time** of an appointment, Outlook takes account of its **Start time**.

⇨ Convert a message into an appointment by first selecting the message then dragging it into the **Calendar** shortcut in the **Outlook Shortcuts** group.

⇨ By default, days that have appointments, meetings or events are shown in bold.

B-Creating an event

An **event** is an activity which lasts at least 24 hours. It does not occupy a particular slot in the Diary pane.

- Display the Calendar, and activate the day on which the event starts.
- **Actions - New All Day Event**

Microsoft Outlook 2000

① Indicate what the event is and where it is to take place.
② If necessary, fill in the start and end dates of the event.
③ Confirm.

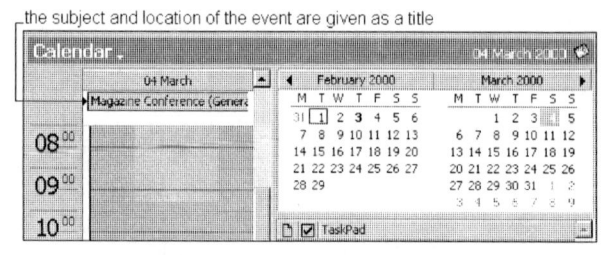

⇨ To change an event into an appointment as you are creating it, deactivate the *All day event* option.

⇨ Double-click the event title in the Diary pane to activate the **Event** window.

C-Managing items

▧ To change an item in the Diary pane, double-click the item. Make your changes then click [Save and Close].

When only the item's subject has to be modified just click the item once and it can be modified right away; when you have modified it press [Enter].

▧ When deleting an item select it, keeping the [Ctrl] button pressed down if there is more than one item.

▧ Edit
　Delete　　　　　　　　　[X]　　　　　　　　　　[Ctrl] D

If you have selected several items you can use the [Del] *key. When you delete an item which recurs, Outlook will ask you if just the selected item is to be deleted or if every occurrence is to be deleted.*

If you happen to delete some items by mistake you can cancel the operation by ***Edit - Undo*** *or* [Ctrl] ***Z****. You can also retrieve lost items from the* ***Deleted Items*** *folder.*

- To move an item, position the mouse pointer to its left and select it.

  When the pointer resembles a ✥ drag the item to the new time slot (on the Diary pane) or to the new date (in the Date Navigator).

D-Repeating an item

- When creating or modifying the item use:

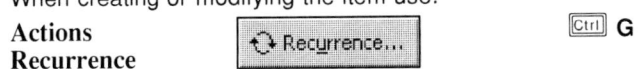

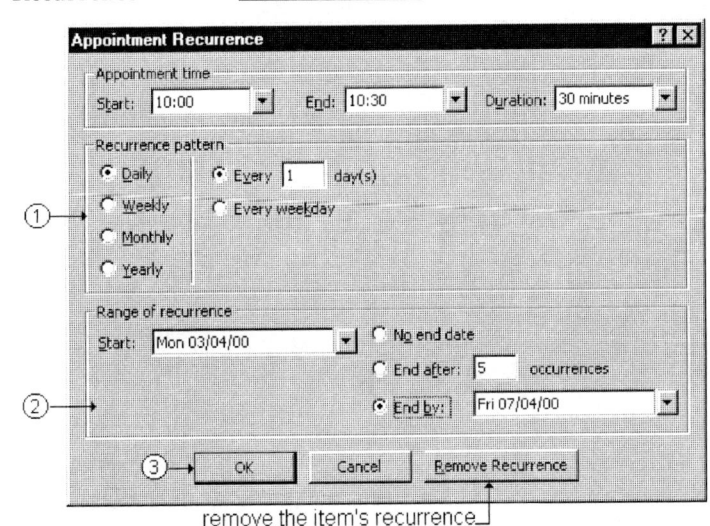

  Actions
  Recurrence   ↻ Recurrence...   [Ctrl] **G**

Appointment Recurrence dialog box:
- Appointment time: Start: 10:00, End: 10:30, Duration: 30 minutes
- Recurrence pattern (①): Daily, Weekly, Monthly, Yearly / Every 1 day(s), Every weekday
- Range of recurrence (②): Start: Mon 03/04/00; No end date / End after: 5 occurrences / End by: Fri 07/04/00
- ③ OK | Cancel | Remove Recurrence — *remove the item's recurrence*

① Indicate the frequency of the repetition.

② Indicate the period of time over which the item is to be repeated.

③ Confirm.

➭ *To view only* ***Recurring Appointments****, select the corresponding view.*

➭ *You can also create a recurring item (appointment, event or meeting) by activating the appropriate option in the* ***Actions*** *menu.*

Microsoft Outlook 2000

E-Setting an alarm

The purpose of the alarm is to remind you at regular intervals of appointments, events or meetings.

Go into the item in which the alarm is to be set.

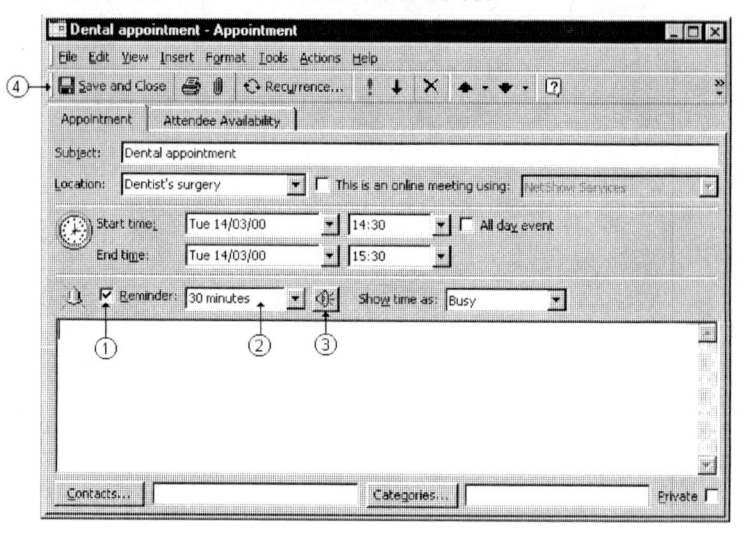

① Activate this option.

② Indicate by how much time the alarm is to precede the item.

③ Define a sound which will accompany the reminder.

④ Enter.

▷ In the daily and weekly views, the items accompanied by an alarm are marked with this symbol.

▷ To cancel an alarm, go into the item and deactivate the **Reminder** option.

▷ By default, alarms are set off a quarter of an hour before the item is due to begin. To remove or change this setting, use **Tools - Options - Preferences** tab.

⇨ When the alarm is set off, Outlook displays a dialog box to remind you of the item's subject and location.

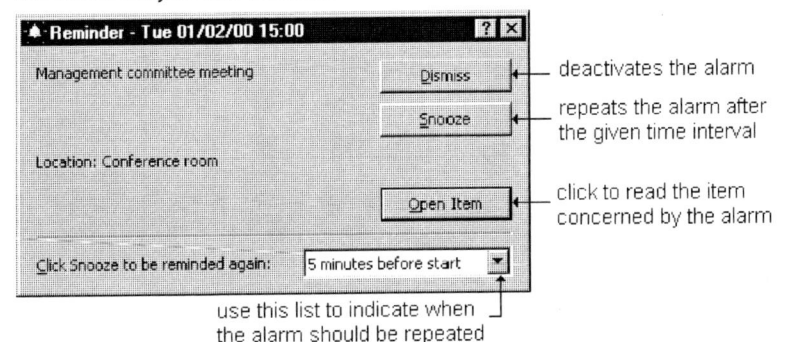

- deactivates the alarm
- repeats the alarm after the given time interval
- click to read the item concerned by the alarm
- use this list to indicate when the alarm should be repeated

F- Defining your availability

This allows users consulting your schedule to know when you are available.

■ When creating or modifying an item open the **Show time as** list and choose one of the options.

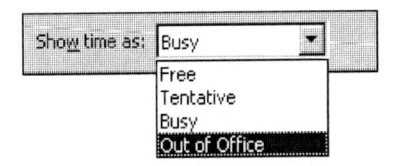

The item will appear in a different colour according to the option chosen: *Free* (pale or transparent), *Tentative* (sky blue), *Busy* (blue), *Out of Office* (violet).

⇨ The free/busy information is updated automatically for 2 months, every 15 minutes. To change these options, use **Tools - Options**, click the **Calendar options** button then the **Free/Busy options** button to change the number of months of information published and frequency of updates.

⇨ To publish your availability information on the Internet, go to the **Free/Busy Options** dialog box, activate the **Publish my free/busy information** check box and, in the **Publish at this URL** box give the address of the server on which your availability information is to be stored.

Microsoft Outlook 2000

3.3 Meetings

A-Creating a meeting

A meeting is an appointment which involves other people.

- Display the Calendar.
- Select the day of the meeting, and if possible, its start time or the period of time involved.
- Actions
  Plan a Meeting
- Click the **Invite Others** button.

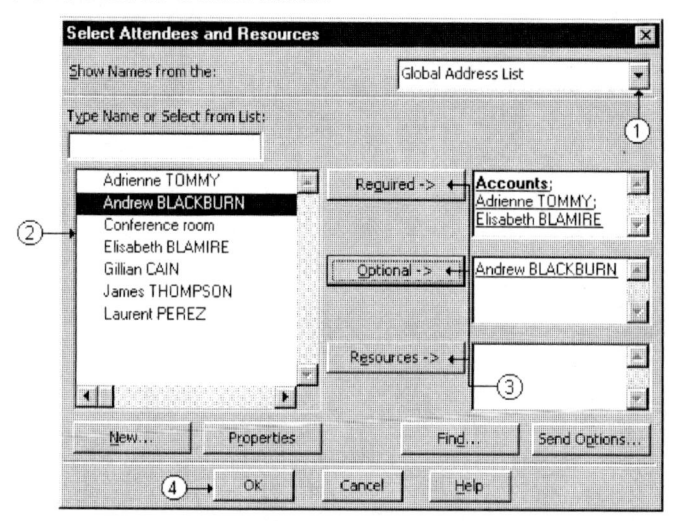

① Select the address book from which you wish to invite participants.
② Select each participant's name.
③ Indicate whether his/her presence is required or optional, or if the item selected is a resource.
④ Confirm.

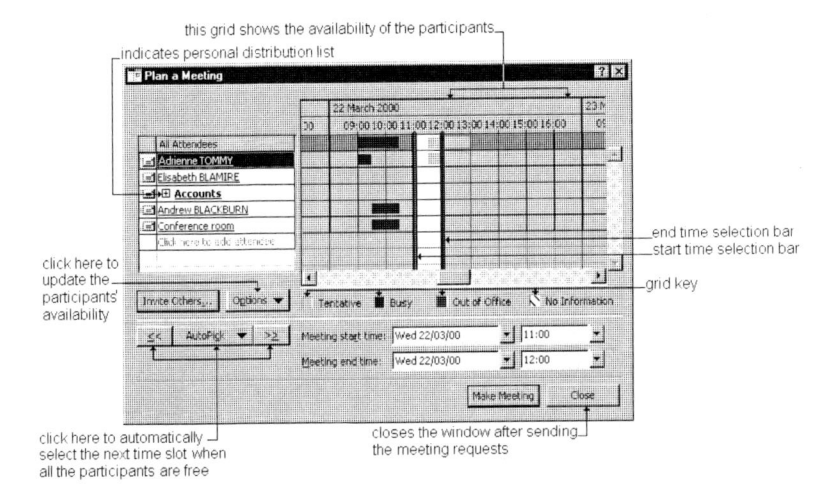

this grid shows the availability of the participants
indicates personal distribution list

end time selection bar
start time selection bar
click here to update the participants' availability
grid key
click here to automatically select the next time slot when all the participants are free
closes the window after sending the meeting requests

▨ Use the **Meeting start time** and **Meeting end time** options to indicate the time of the meeting or drag the meeting selection bars in the grid you could also click the **AutoPick** button.

▨ Click the **Make Meeting** button.

▨ Enter details concerning the meeting then send the meeting invitation and close the **Plan a Meeting** window.

⇨ *If you wish to expand a distribution list in order to see all the members, and be able to delete the meeting request to selected members, click the + sign before it.*

⇨ *A resource is a material item (a meeting room or overhead projector, for example) that is represented on your network by a mailbox which is managed by an administrator. This person can schedule and configure the resource so that meeting requests are accepted or declined according to the resource's availability.*

⇨ *In the Calendar's Diary pane a meeting item is marked with this symbol*

⇨ *The ▨ icon, to the left of the each name, indicates that he/she will receive an invitation. If you do not want to send an invitation to a particular participant click this icon then **Don't send meeting to this attendee**.*

B-Selecting contacts before creating a meeting

▨ In the Outlook bar, open the **Outlook Shortcuts** group and click the **Contacts** shortcut.

▨ Select the participants, holding down ⇧ Shift or Ctrl as you click.

▨ **Actions**
   New Meeting with Contact

Microsoft Outlook 2000   43

C-Replying to a request to attend a meeting

▪ In the Calendar, double-click the meeting item, or double-click the corresponding message in the Inbox.

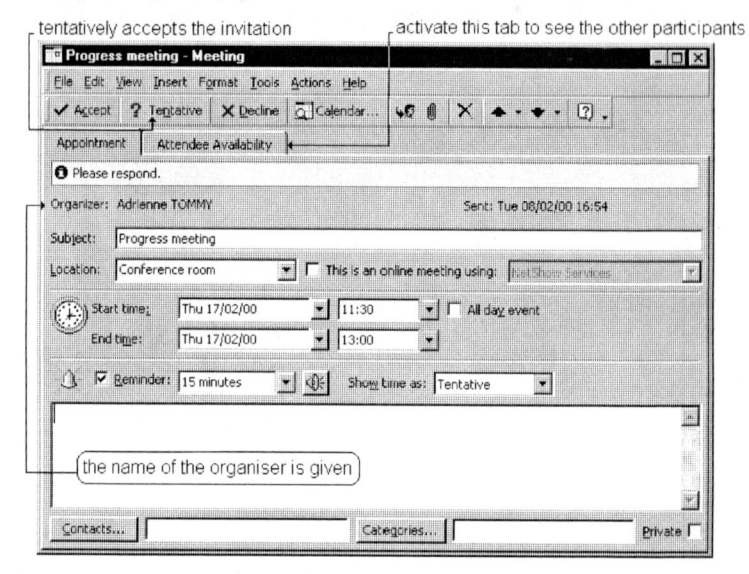

[Screenshot of Progress meeting - Meeting dialog box with annotations: "tentatively accepts the invitation" pointing to Tentative button, "activate this tab to see the other participants" pointing to Attendee Availability tab, "the name of the organiser is given" pointing to Organizer field]

This dialog box appears if you open the meeting item from the Calendar.

▪ Reply by clicking **Accept**, **Tentative** or **Decline**.

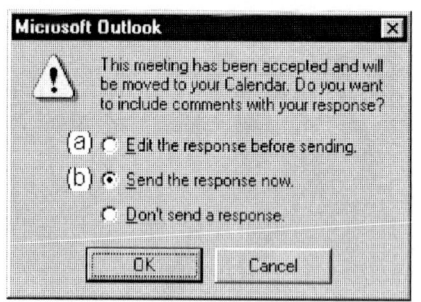

[Screenshot of Microsoft Outlook dialog: "This meeting has been accepted and will be moved to your Calendar. Do you want to include comments with your response?" with options (a) Edit the response before sending, (b) Send the response now, Don't send a response]

▪ Choose one of the following options:
   (a)   add a comment to your reply
   (b)   send the reply without comment

▪ If you wish to add a comment to your reply enter it then click the **Send** button.

D-Viewing the replies to a meeting request

- Go into your Inbox and open each reply that you have received.
- In the Calendar, open the meeting to which other users have been invited. On the **Appointment** page Outlook displays a summary of all the replies.

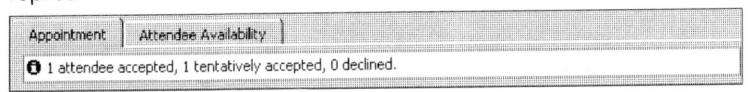

> Appointment | Attendee Availability
> 🛈 1 attendee accepted, 1 tentatively accepted, 0 declined.

- On the **Attendee Availability** page activate the **Show attendee status** option to display the report as it applies to individual participants.

E-Adding/withdrawing a request to attend

- Double-click the meeting in question (if it is a recurring meeting, indicate whether all the meetings are concerned or only the current meeting).
- **Actions - Add or Remove Attendees**

    The *Select Attendees and Resources* dialog box appears.

- To cancel a participant's invitation, click his or her name in one of the right-hand columns and press [Del].
- To add attendees (or resources), select them from the address lists and add them to the **Required, Optional** and **Resources** boxes.
- Click **OK** then [Save and Close].

F-Cancelling a meeting

- Select the meeting to be cancelled.
- **Edit**   [X]   [Ctrl] **D**
  Delete

    You can also open the meeting and use Actions - Cancel meeting.

- If it is a recurring meeting indicate whether just this particular meeting is to be cancelled or the whole series.
- Indicate whether a cancellation notice should be sent to each participant.

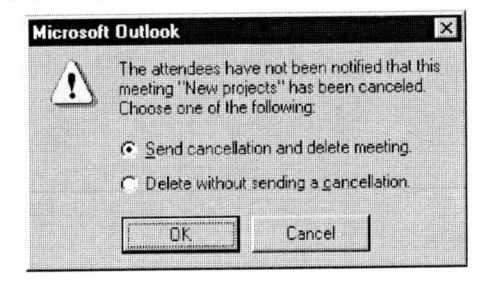

> **Microsoft Outlook**
> ⚠ The attendees have not been notified that this meeting "New projects" has been canceled. Choose one of the following:
> ● Send cancellation and delete meeting.
> ○ Delete without sending a cancellation.
> [OK] [Cancel]

Microsoft Outlook 2000

G-Creating an online meeting

This technique uses NetShow Services and Microsoft NetMeeting (which requires the active participation of the people concerned) to allow you to communicate with several users over the Internet or by using your company's intranet.

▪ **File - New - Meeting Request** or Ctrl Shift **Q**

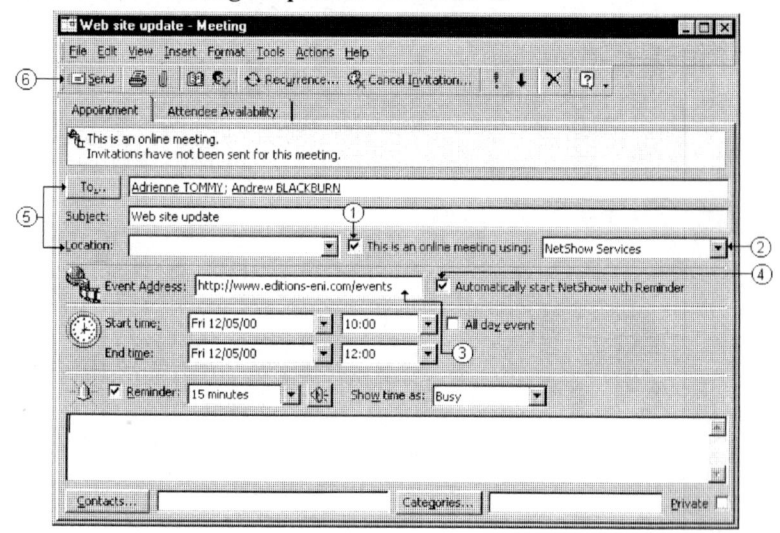

①Activate this option.

②Indicate which program you want to use **Microsoft NetMeeting** or **NetShow Services**.

③If you have chosen to use Microsoft NetMeeting, give the **Directory Server** name; if you have chosen NetShow Services, enter the URL address of the event.

④Activate this option if you want the application to start automatically and show a reminder.

⑤Define the other information for the meeting.

⑥Send the invitation.

▷ *If you have not chosen to have the application run automatically, participate in the meeting by right-clicking the meeting in the Calendar and choosing* **Start NetMeeting** *(for a NetMeeting) or* **View NetShow** *(for a NetShow).*

3.4 Printing a Calendar

A-Printing

- Go into the **Calendar** then activate, if necessary, the **Day/Week/Month** view.
- **File**
  Print   `Ctrl` **P**

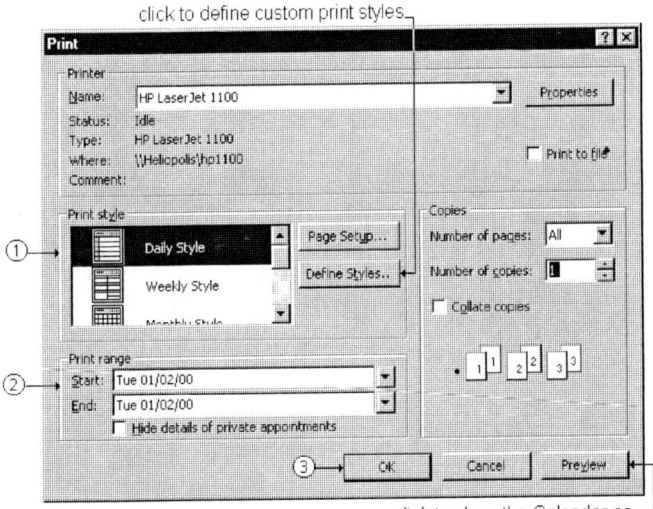

click to define custom print styles

① *(Print style selection)*

② *(Print range)*

③ *(OK button)*

click to show the Calendar as it will look when printed

① Choose your print style:

Daily Style	One day per page with space for tasks and notes.
Weekly Style	One week per page with space for tasks and notes.
Monthly Style	One month per page without space for tasks and notes.
Tri-fold Style	Three clearly defined sections comprising one day, one month and a task list, all printed on the same page so that it can be folded in three equal parts.
Calendar Details Style	One day per page, without space for tasks but with details of the appointments.

② Indicate the period of time to be printed.

③ Start printing.

Microsoft Outlook 2000

B-Previewing the Calendar

- Select the time period you want to see if necessary.
- **File**
  Print Preview

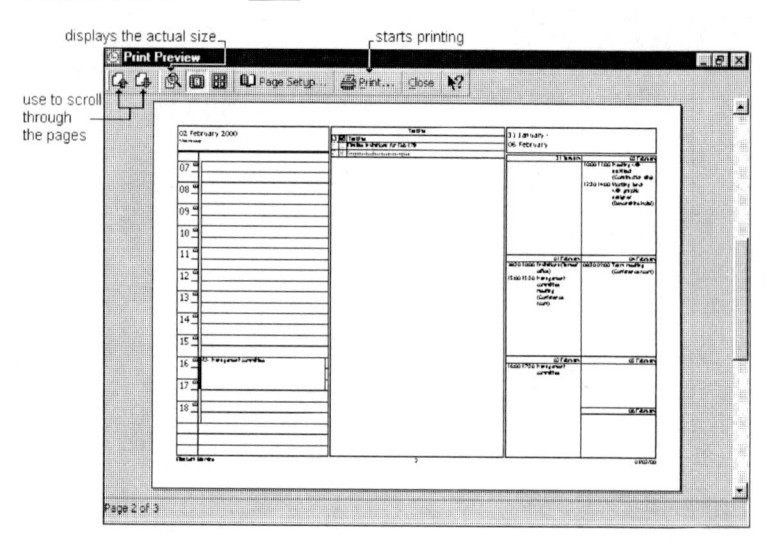

C-Printing Calendar items

- Go into the Calendar.
- Select the items to be printed (hold down the `Ctrl` key as you click to select several items).
- **File**
  Print   `Ctrl` **P**
- Choose the **Memo Style** in the **Print style** frame.
- Indicate whether you wish to **Start each item on a new page**.
- If you want to print the contents of any attachments, activate the **Print attached files with item(s)** option.
- Click **OK**.

48

3.5 Configuring the Calendar

A-Defining the working week and working hours

By default, Outlook proposes a working week from Monday to Friday, with working days from 8:00 to 17:00.

- **Tools - Options - Preferences** tab
- Click the **Calendar Options** button.

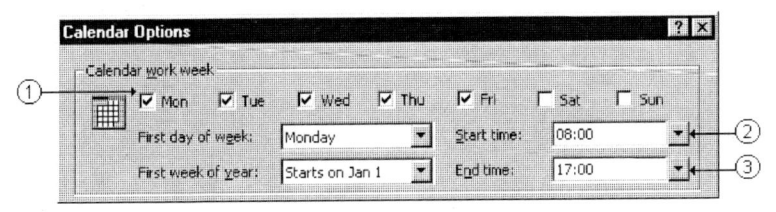

① Tick the working days and deactivate the non-working days.
② Select the first working hour.
③ Select the end of the working day.

B-Changing the Date Navigator view

- To show week numbers in the Date Navigator, use **Tools - Options - Preferences** tab. Click the **Calendar Options** button and activate the **Show week numbers in the Date Navigator** option in the **Calendar options** frame.

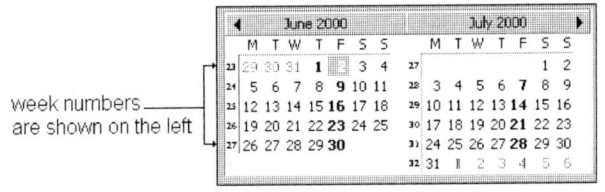

week numbers are shown on the left

- To change the font used in the Date Navigator, use **Tools - Options - Other** tab. Click the **Advanced Options** button in the **General** frame then click **Font** in the **Appearance options** frame. Choose the **Font, Font style** and **Size**.

- To change the appearance of days containing items, use **View - Current View - Customize Current View** and click the **Other Settings** button. Deactivate the **Bolded dates in Date Navigator represent days containing items** option.

⇨ *For Outlook, the first week of the year is that which contains the first of January. If this setting is not convenient, define the characteristics of the First week of year in the Calendar Options dialog box (Tools - Options).*

Microsoft Outlook 2000

4.1 Outlook Today

*The **Outlook Today** page gives you a quick picture of all your appointments during the next few days, as well as the number of messages you have received, and a task list.*

A- Going into Outlook Today

- In the **Outlook** bar, open the **Outlook Shortcuts** and click **Outlook Today**.

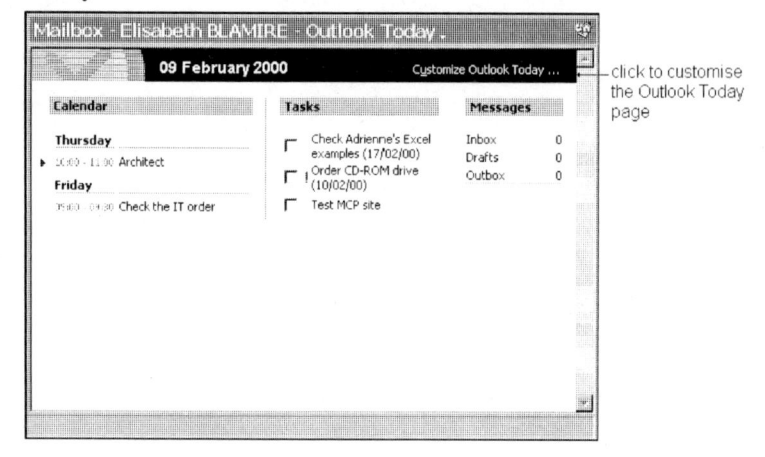

click to customise the Outlook Today page

B-Customising the Outlook Today page

■ In the **Outlook Today** page, click **Customize Outlook Today**.

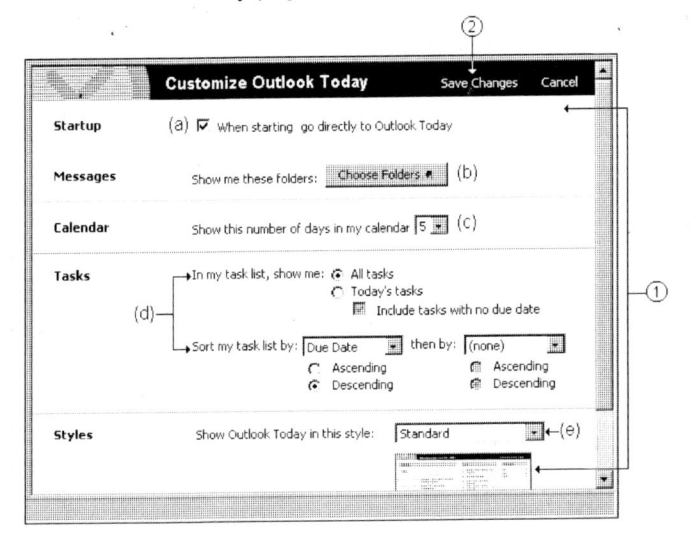

```
                                                    ②
┌─────────────────────────────────────────────────────┐
│   Customize Outlook Today      Save Changes  Cancel │
│                                                     │
│ Startup    (a) ☑ When starting go directly to Outlook Today │
│                                                     │
│ Messages   Show me these folders: [Choose Folders]  (b) │
│                                                     │
│ Calendar   Show this number of days in my calendar [5]  (c) │
│                                                     │
│ Tasks      → In my task list, show me: ⊙ All tasks  │
│                                        ○ Today's tasks │
│            (d)                         ☑ Include tasks with no due date   ──① │
│            → Sort my task list by: [Due Date]  then by: [(none)] │
│                    ○ Ascending              ○ Ascending │
│                    ⊙ Descending             ⊙ Descending │
│                                                     │
│ Styles     Show Outlook Today in this style: [Standard]  ←(e) │
│                                                     │
└─────────────────────────────────────────────────────┘
```

① Make your changes:
  (a) activate this option to show the Outlook Today page automatically when you open Outlook.
  (b) select the folders for which you want to see the number of new messages in the Outlook Today page.
  (c) indicate how many calendar days you want to see.
  (d) choose whether you want to see all your tasks or only those for today. How should the task list be sorted?
  (e) use this list to choose a view for the Outlook Today page.

② Return to the Outlook Today page by saving your changes.

Microsoft Outlook 2000

4.2 The Contacts folder

The **Contacts** folder enables you to store all kinds of information concerning your business contacts, including names, addresses, telephone numbers...

A- Going into the Contacts folder

▓ Open the **Outlook Shortcuts** group in the Outlook bar and click the **Contacts** shortcut.

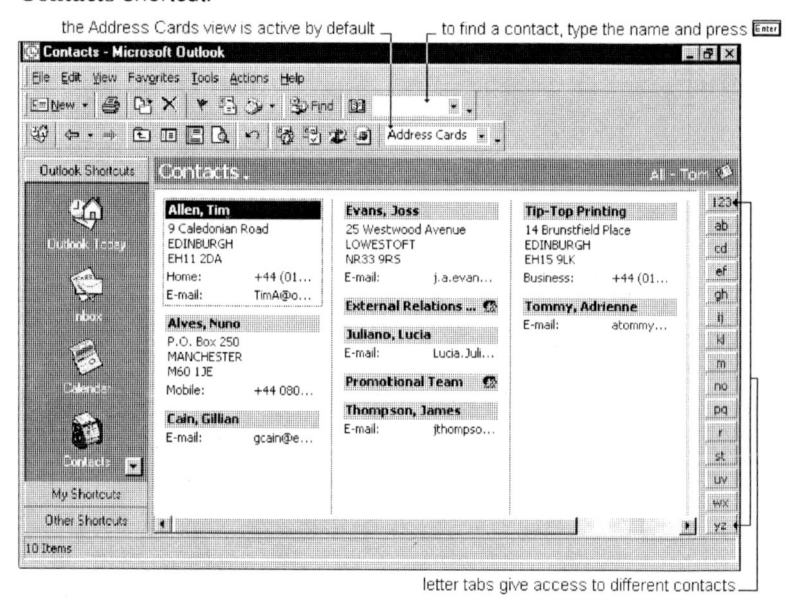

the Address Cards view is active by default

to find a contact, type the name and press Enter

letter tabs give access to different contacts

B-Creating a contact

▓ **File - New - Contact** or Ctrl + Shift C
or
Go to the **Contacts** folder and click the **New** button on the Standard toolbar or choose **File - New - Contact** (Ctrl N) or **Actions - New Contact**.

■ On the **General** tab, enter your contact's details:

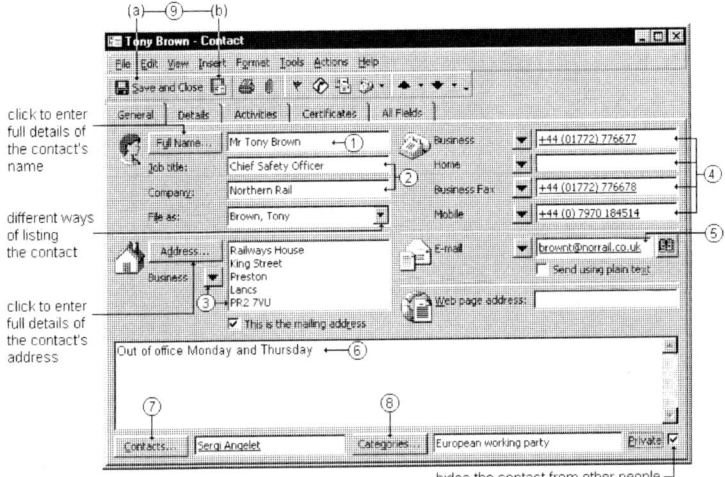

click to enter full details of the contact's name

different ways of listing the contact

click to enter full details of the contact's address

hides the contact from other people with access to the folder

① Enter the contact's name.
② Enter his/her title (Mr. Mrs. Dr. ...) and the name of the company.
③ Indicate whether the address is **Business**, **Home** or **Other** then enter it. You can then choose to enter another address if you wish.
④ Enter the various telephone numbers.
⑤ Enter e-mail details.
⑥ Enter any necessary contacts.
⑦ If necessary, link the current contact (main contact) to other contacts.
⑧ Indicate the category in which the contact is to be filed.
⑨ Confirm:
  (a) by closing the window.
  (b) by opening another window for a new contact.

The **Details** tab can be used to add extra information about the contact's job, personal details or the contact's NetMeeting server.

⇨ The **Activities** tab shows all the items associated with the contact (messages, appointments, tasks).

⇨ By default, contacts are displayed on address cards; these cards are classified first by surname, then by first name, in the **Contacts** folder.

⇨ When you double-click the contact's name you open the **Contact** window.

⇨ If you need to add a contact to a company which is already in the **Contacts** folder, select another contact from the same company and use the **Actions - New Contact from Same Company** command. All the details (name, address, telephone) concerning the company are automatically recalled and you have only to enter personal details then save this new contact.

Microsoft Outlook 2000

C-Calling a contact

This function is only available if you have a modem; in addition, both your PC and your modem must be configured for automatic dialling.

- Select the contact whom you wish to telephone from your contacts list.
- **Actions - Call Contact**

click the number you want to dial

- If you want to make a note of this call in your Journal, activate the **Create new Journal Entry when starting new call** option in the **New call** window.
- Click the **Start Call** button.

If you are making a note of the call, the Journal Entry window appears, so that you can make notes and start the timer.

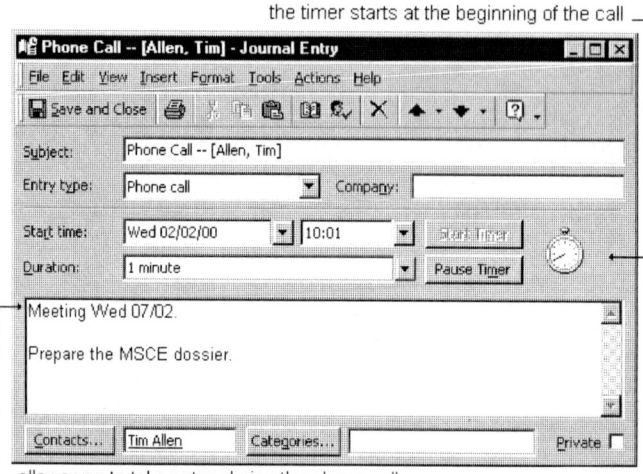

the timer starts at the beginning of the call

allows you to take notes during the phone call

- Make your call.
- When you have finished, click the **Pause Timer** button, if necessary, then close the Journal Entry window.
- Hang up the receiver and click the **End Call** button.

⇨ *If you were unable to reach your correspondent, try again using the Actions - Call Contact - Redial command.*

D-Creating a Speed Dial List

This is a particularly useful feature for those contacts you telephone regularly.

- To create a speed dial list, use:
- **Actions**
  Call Contact
  Speed Dial
  [Ctrl] [⇧ Shift] D
- Click the **Dialing Options** button.

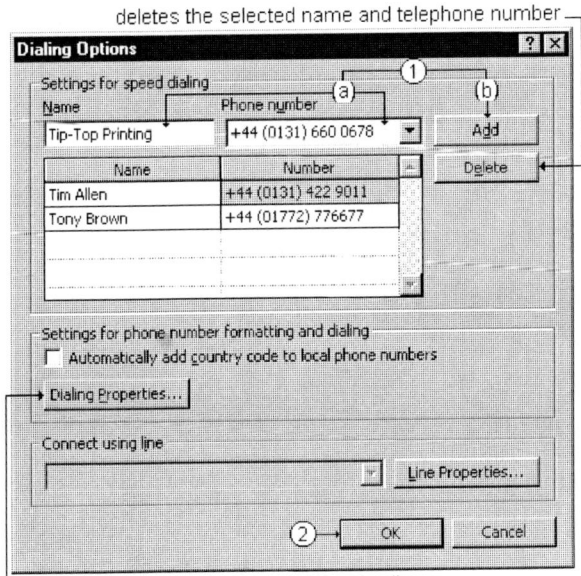

deletes the selected name and telephone number

Dialing Options

Settings for speed dialing
Name — (a) — Phone number — (b)
Tip-Top Printing | +44 (0131) 660 0678 | Add

Name	Number
Tim Allen	+44 (0131) 422 9011
Tony Brown	+44 (01772) 776677

Delete

Settings for phone number formatting and dialing
☐ Automatically add country code to local phone numbers
→ Dialing Properties...

Connect using line
Line Properties...

(2) → OK   Cancel

click for details concerning location of caller, area codes, international codes

① For each contact:
  (a) enter the details.
  (b) confirm.

② Confirm.

- Close the call window by clicking **Close**.
- To call a contact who is already saved in your speed dialling list, use **Actions - Call Contact - Speed Dial**, and click the appropriate number.

Microsoft Outlook 2000

E- Setting a follow up flag for a contact

- Go into the **Contacts** folder.
- Choose the contact for whom you wish to set a reminder.
- **Actions**
  Flag for Follow Up   `Ctrl` `⇧ Shift` **G**

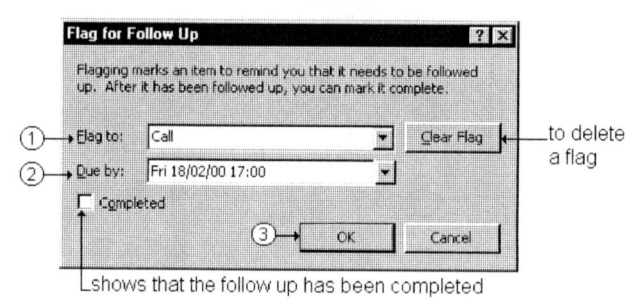

①→ Flag to
②→ Due by
to delete a flag
③→ OK
shows that the follow up has been completed

① Choose the follow-up action to take.
② Give the date and time of the reminder.
③ Click to confirm.

⇨ When you use **Flag for Follow Up View**, all the contacts are grouped according to their flag status.

⇨ When the reminder time comes, a **Reminder** dialog box appears.

⇨ When you open a contact's window (by double-clicking their name), you can see the follow-up action in the **General** tab.

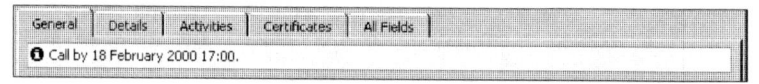

| General | Details | Activities | Certificates | All Fields |

❶ Call by 18 February 2000 17:00.

⇨ Once the follow-up is completed do not forget to activate the **Completed** option in the **Flag for Follow Up** dialog box.

F- Managing links with a contact

Contacts are of course directly linked to an item when they are connected, but you can also choose to link a contact to any existing item, or one you are creating.

- When you are creating an item, click the **Contacts** button in the creation dialog box (for messages, click the **Options** button first) then select the contacts to be linked to the item.
- To link an existing item to a contact, open the contact and use **Actions - Link - Items**.

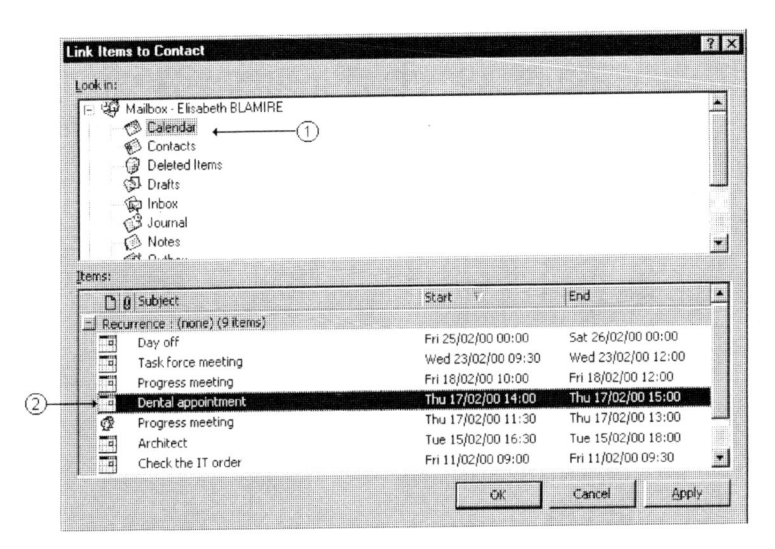

① Select the folder that contains the item.

② Click the item.

To show the items linked to a contact, open the contact in question, and click the **Activities** tab.

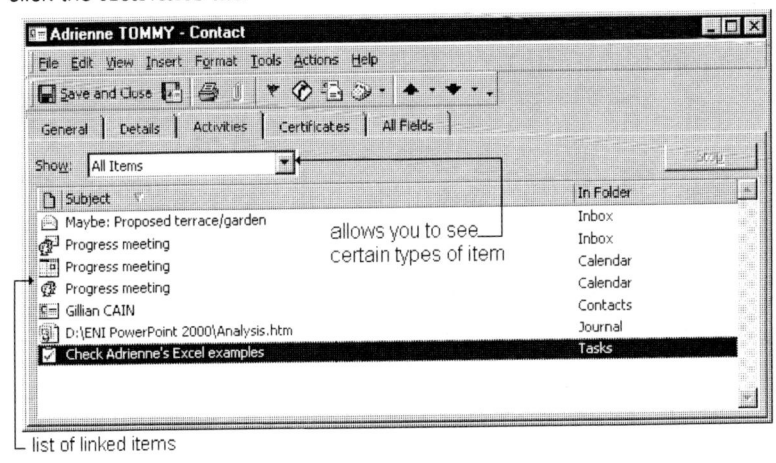

list of linked items

G-Printing your contacts

- Go into your **Contacts** folder.
- If necessary, select the contacts to be printed.
- **File**
  Print   `Ctrl` P

to define headers and footers

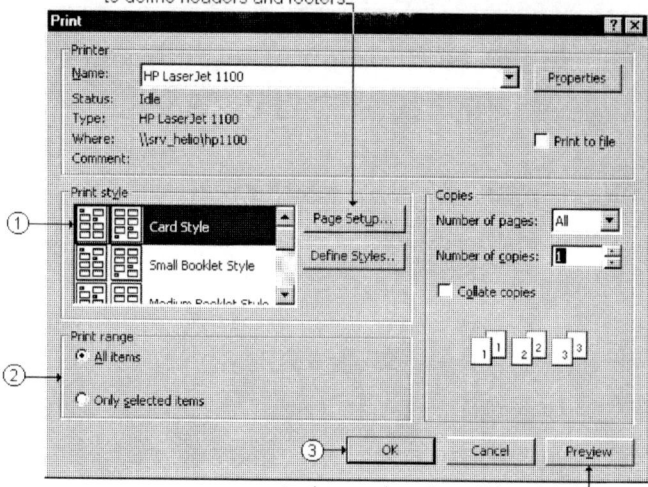

to show cards as they will be printed

① Choose the most suitable style from the following list:

Card Style — All the cards are printed one after the other from top to bottom in a column.

Small Booklet Style — All the cards are printed on both sides of a sheet of paper, making eight pages in all, in landscape orientation.

Medium Booklet Style — All the cards are printed on both sides of a sheet of paper, making four pages on a sheet, in portrait orientation.

Memo Style — Only selected items are printed, one at a time, in the form of an e-mail message.

Phone Directory Style — The names and telephone numbers of all the contacts are printed from top to bottom of the page.

② Choose the print range for the items. If you choose **Memo Style**, only the selected items will be printed, and in this case, the **Print range** frame is replaced by a set of **Print options** enabling you to **Start each item on a new page** and/or **Print attached file with item(s)**.

③ Start printing.

H-Creating a distribution list

*A **distribution list** is like a circulation list. When you send a message to the list, all the contacts on that list receive the message at the same time.*

- File - New - Distribution List or Ctrl L

or

Go to the **Contacts** folder and use **Actions - New Distribution List**.

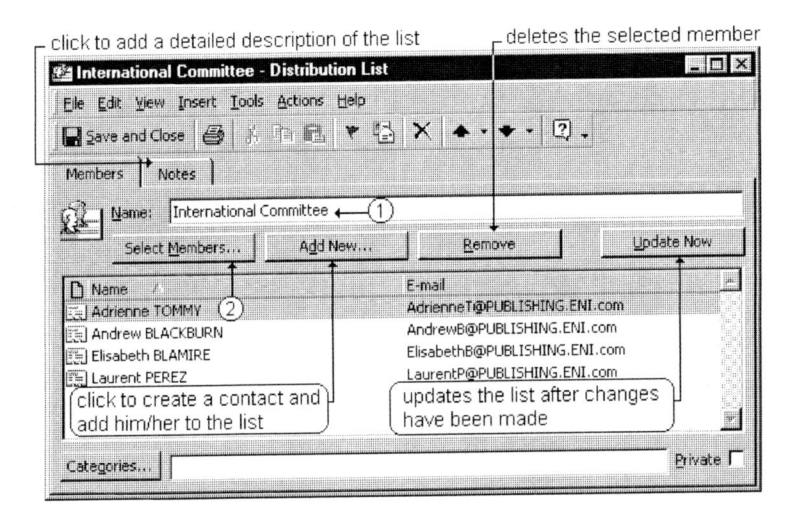

click to add a detailed description of the list — *deletes the selected member*

click to create a contact and add him/her to the list — *updates the list after changes have been made*

① Give a name to the list you are creating.
② Add the contacts you want.

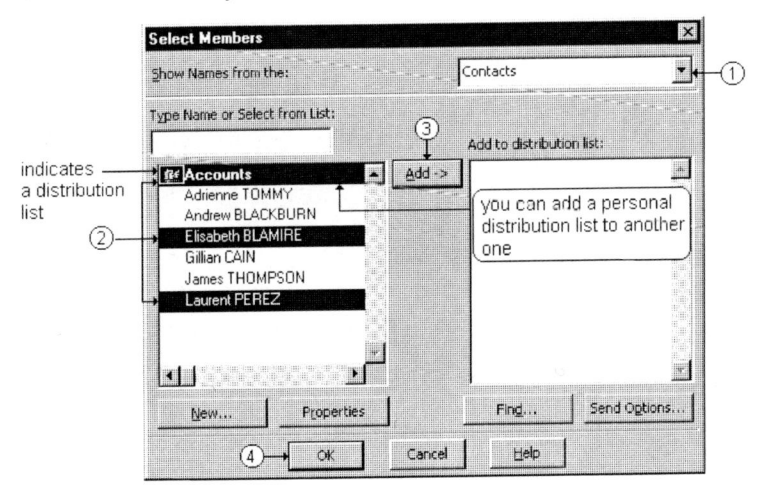

indicates a distribution list

① Choose the address book required.
② Select the members to be included.
③ Add these members to the distribution list.
④ Confirm.

▪ In the **Distribution List** window, click [Save and Close].

⇨ *By default, personal distribution lists are entered in your Contacts folder.*

Microsoft Outlook 2000

I- Discovering the address books

▪ Tools
  Address Book   [Ctrl] [⇧ Shift] B

▪ In the **Show Names from the** list, select the address book you want to use. You may have a choice of several address books:

Global Address List — This list is created and managed by the network administrator. It contains all the e-mail addresses of the mail users, and any distribution lists.

Outlook Address Book — Outlook's own address list, automatically created from the contacts in the **Contacts** folder that contain an e-mail address or fax number.

Contacts — A personal address book that you can customise to suit your needs. Use to store your contacts and distribution lists.

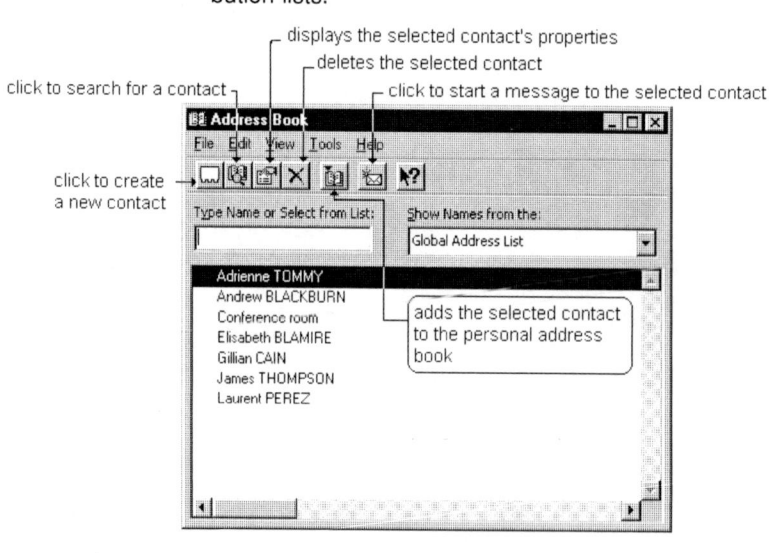

[Screenshot of Address Book window with annotations: "click to search for a contact", "click to create a new contact", "displays the selected contact's properties", "deletes the selected contact", "click to start a message to the selected contact", "adds the selected contact to the personal address book". List shows: Adrienne TOMMY, Andrew BLACKBURN, Conference room, Elisabeth BLAMIRE, Gillian CAIN, James THOMPSON, Laurent PEREZ]

4.3 The Tasks folder

A **task** is a professional or personal obligation to be fulfilled.

A- Viewing tasks

▪ On the **Outlook** bar, click **Outlook Shortcuts** then the **Tasks** folder or the **Calendar** (in **Day/Week/Month** view).

60

double-click this icon to open the Task window

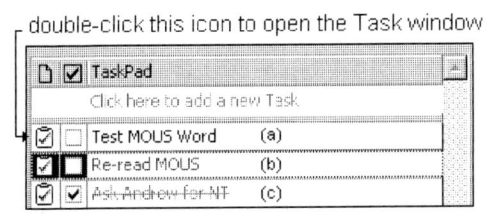

Uncompleted tasks (a) are preceded by an empty square; **Overdue tasks** (b) appear in red; **Completed tasks** (c) are preceded by a tick, appear dim and are scored out.

⇒ You can redefine the colours for *Overdue* and *Completed* tasks by using the list of the same name in the *Task options* dialog box *(Tools - Options - Preferences tab, Task Options button)*.

B-Setting yourself a task

■ **File - New - Task** or `Ctrl` `û Shift` **K**
or
Go to the **Tasks** folder and click the **New** button on the **Standard** toolbar or use **File - New - Task** (`Ctrl` **N**) or **Actions - New Task**.

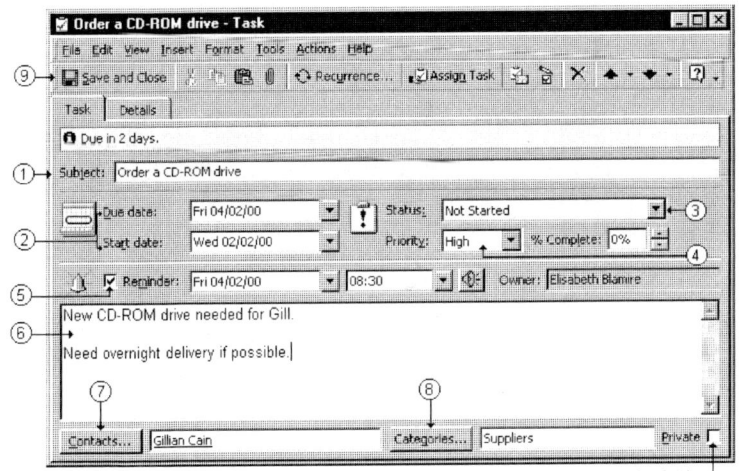

hides the task from other users who can access the folder

① Enter a description of the task.

② Enter both the task's due date and its start date.

③ Indicate the task's state of progress.

④ Give the task a priority rating: **Low**, **Normal** or **High**.

⑤ If necessary, enter details of the date and time when an alarm should be set off.

⑥ Enter details of the task.

⑦ Associate a contact with the task if necessary.

Microsoft Outlook 2000

⑧ If you wish, give the task a category.
⑨ Enter.

⇨ You can create a task by clicking in the **Click here to add a new Task** box in the Calendar's **TaskPad**.

⇨ To change a message into a task, select the message concerned and drag it into the **Tasks** shortcut in the **Outlook Shortcuts** group. Enter details of the task then save it.

C-Assigning a task to somebody else

Go into the task then use the command:
Actions
Assign Task

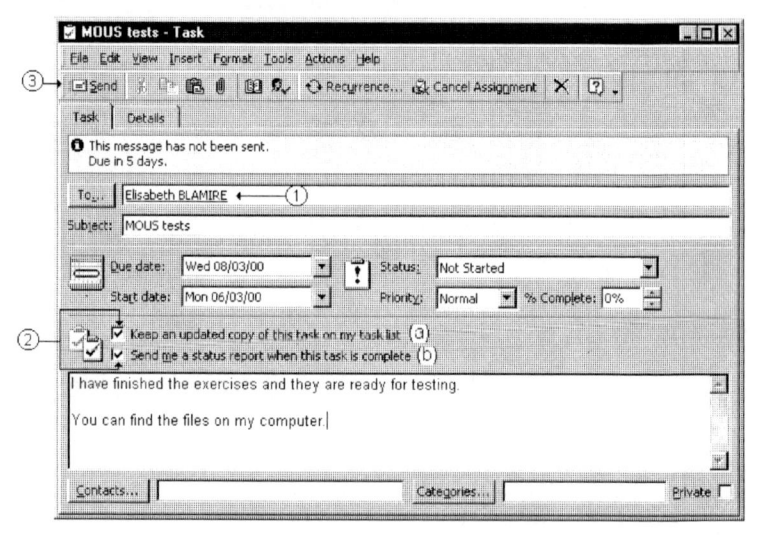

① Indicate the name of the person(s) to whom you wish to assign this task.

② Indicate whether you want to:
  (a) keep a copy of this task in your task list, which will be updated with any changes made by the person(s) to whom you assign the task.
  (b) receive a status report from the person(s) to whom the task has been assigned once it is complete.

③ Send the message.

If a reminder has been set, Outlook informs you that it is now cancelled since you are no longer the task's owner.

If necessary, click **OK**.

The task's originator now sees the task in his **Tasks** folder, preceded by this symbol [icon], and in the **Sent Items** folder the task looks like this [icon] and is preceded by **Task Request**.
The new task owner will see the [icon] symbol, representing a task request, in his **Inbox**.

⇨ To select a contact before assigning a task, click the **Contacts** shortcut in the **Outlook Shortcuts** group and select one or more recipients for the task. Next, use the **Actions - New Task for Contact** command. Create the task message in the usual way then click the [Assign Task] button.

D-Replying to a task request

- Open the message which contains the task request.
- Reply by using one of these three buttons: **Accept**, **Decline** or **Assign Task** to assign the task to somebody else.
- If you do not want to add any comments choose the **Send message now** option, otherwise activate **Edit the response before sending**.

When a task is accepted, the task request disappears from the **Inbox** and reappears in the **Task** folder, preceded by this symbol [icon], and also in the **Sent Items** folder, preceded by this symbol [icon]. You are now the task owner.
Any tasks that you refuse appear in the **Sent Items** folder, accompanied by the [icon] symbol. Once a task is refused, it no longer has an owner!
The original task owner sees the [icon] and [icon] symbols in his **Inbox**.

E-Creating a recurring task

- Create or modify the task concerned then use:
  Actions   [Recurrence...]   [Ctrl] G
  Recurrence

Microsoft Outlook 2000

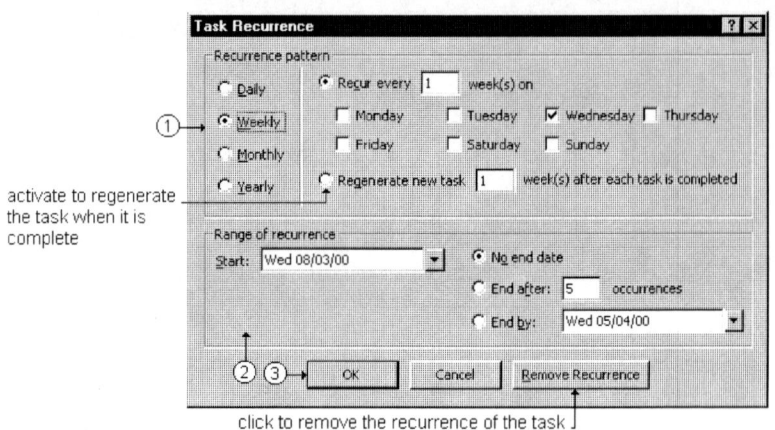

activate to regenerate the task when it is complete

click to remove the recurrence of the task

① Determine the frequency of the task.

② Enter details of the task's start date and duration.

③ Enter.

F-Reporting on a task's progress

Only the task owner can give information about how a task is progressing.

▪ Open the task concerned.

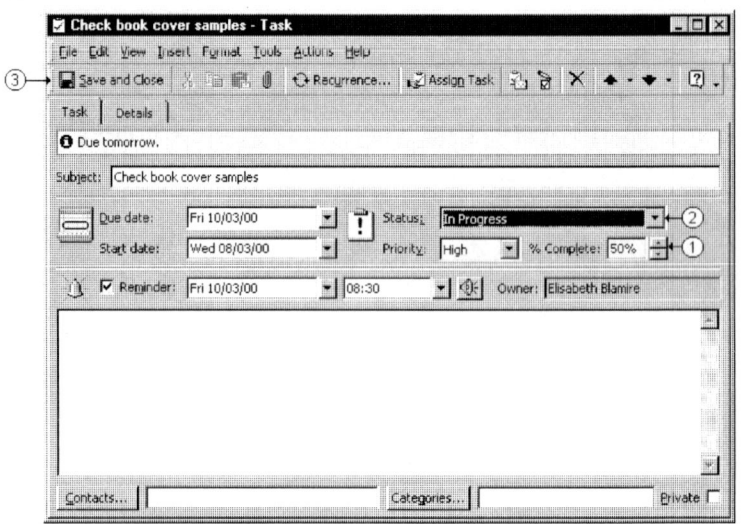

① Enter the percentage of progress achieved and press Enter (as soon as you confirm, **In Progress** appears in the **Status** list).

② You can change the status of the task's progress: **Deferred**, or **Waiting on somebody else**.

③ Enter.

⇨ To indicate that the task is complete, enter *100* in *% Complete*, or select *Completed* in the status list, or simply click the ⬜ button. If you want to view only completed tasks activate the *Completed Tasks* view.

⇨ If the task has been assigned to you by somebody else, that person will automatically be informed of the task's completion.

⇨ You do not have to open a task to declare it complete, just click the square in front of it!

G-Defining tracking options

▪ Create the task then go into **File - Properties**.

▪ On the **General** page, activate **Read receipt requested** and/or **Delivery receipt requested** as appropriate.

4.4 The Notes folder

Notes are the electronic equivalent of Post-it ® notes. This folder enables you to note down any points: questions, ideas or instructions which you need to remember, or to make a note of text that you intend to use elsewhere.

A-Using the Notes folder

▪ In the **Outlook** bar, open the **Outlook Shortcuts** group and click the **Notes** shortcut.

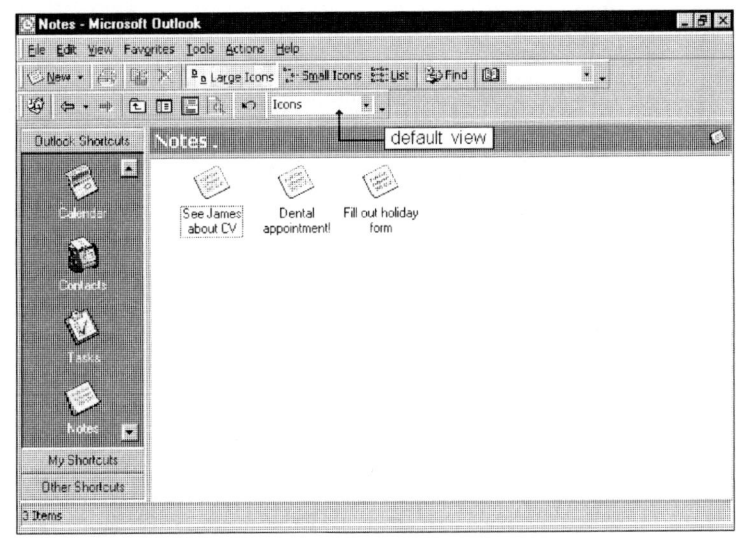

Microsoft Outlook 2000

B-Creating a note

- File - New - Note or [Ctrl][⇧ Shift] W
  or
  Go to the **Notes** folder and click the **New** button on the **Standard** toolbar, or File - New - Note ([Ctrl] N), or Actions - New Note)
- Enter the note text then click [X] to close the window.
- ⇨ *To create a note from another item, select the text to be included in the note: this might be the subject or the whole text of an item. Then drag the selection to the Notes shortcut.*

C-Reading/modifying a note

- Double-click the note in the **Notes** folder.
- Read or modify the note as any other text.
- Close the note by clicking the [X] button.

D-Forwarding a note to other users

- Select the note to be forwarded.
- **Actions - Forward** or [Ctrl] **F**
- Select the name(s) of the user(s) to receive the note.
- Click the [=] **Send** button.
  Notes are forwarded in the form of a message.

E-Changing the characteristics of a note

- **Tools - Options**
  Preferences tab
- Click the **Notes Options** button.

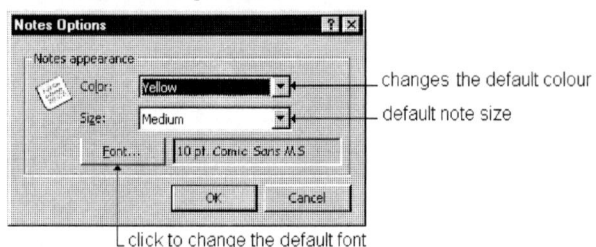

Notes Options dialog:
- Color: Yellow — changes the default colour
- Size: Medium — default note size
- Font... 10 pt Comic Sans MS
- click to change the default font

⇨ *To hide the date and time, which appear in the note window automatically, deactivate **When viewing Notes, show time and date** in the Advanced Options dialog box (**Tools - Options - Other** tab - **Advanced Options** button).*

F-Modifying the notes window size

- Open the note concerned.
- Position the pointer on one edge of the note window.

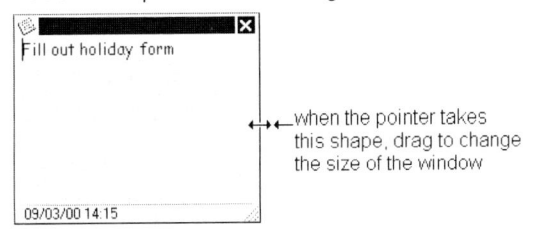

⇨ *Outlook stores this change in its memory.*
⇨ *By default, all new notes appear in a medium-sized window. To change this option, use the Size list in the Options dialog box (Tools - Options - Preferences tab - Note Options button).*

G-Modifying the Icons view

- If necessary, activate the **Icons** view.
- **View - Current View - Customize Current View**
  Other Settings button

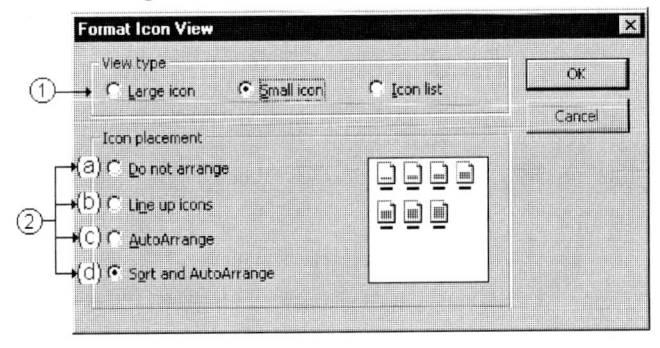

① Choose the view.
② Choose one of the following options:
- (a) the icons stay where you put them.
- (b) aligns the icons on an invisible grid. When you move one of them, it snaps to the nearest point on the grid.
- (c) aligns the icons in several rows.
- (d) aligns the icons in several lines according to current sort criteria.

⇨ *You can also drag notes to move them around.*
⇨ *You cannot choose a placement option if you have activated the Icon List view.*
⇨ *The three view options are also accessible in the View menu.*

4.5 The Journal folder

The Outlook Journal is designed to keep track of all the communications you make on your PC: telephone calls, messages and all Outlook items. It also tracks Office documents, logging details of their creation and modification. Among other things, the Journal records where they are stored.

A-Going to the Journal

- In the **Outlook** bar, open the **My Shortcuts** group and click **Journal**.
- If no automatic Journal entries have been made, Outlook displays this dialog box:

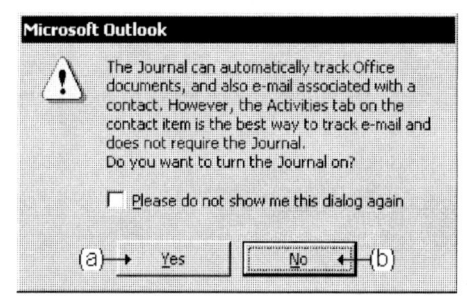

- Choose:
    - (a)   to see the **Journal Options** dialog box and define your automatic entries.
    - (b)   to see the existing journal entries.

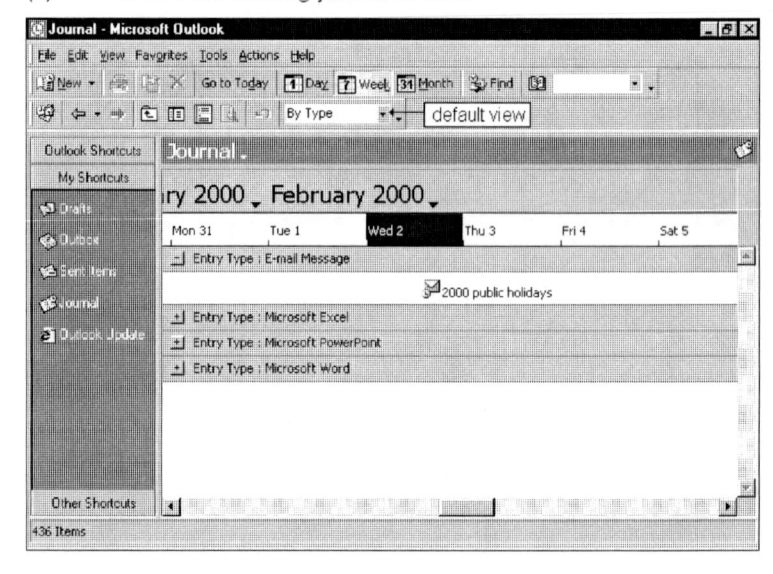

B-Creating a Journal entry manually

- Open or select the item to be included in the Journal.
- Drag the item to the **Journal** shortcut or [Ctrl] **J**.

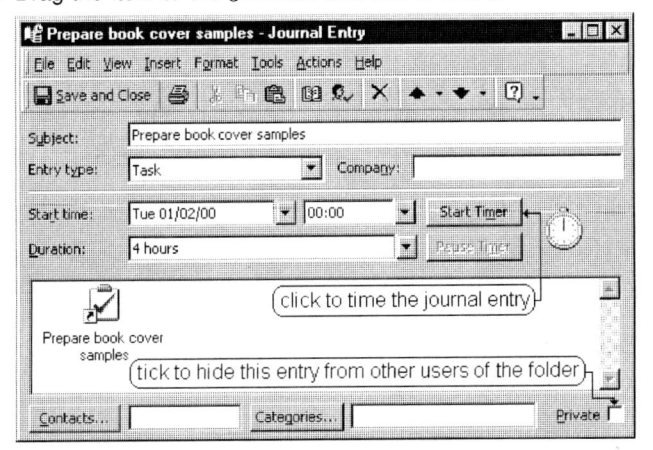

- If necessary, modify existing details (subject, item type).
- Carry out the actions associated with the journal entry.
- Click the **Save and Close** button.

⇨ You can also create a Journal entry without starting an existing item by using the **File - New - Journal Entry** command, [Ctrl][⇧ Shift] **J** or . If the Journal is already open, you can use **Actions - New Journal Entry** or [Ctrl] **N**.

C-Creating automatic entries

- Go to the **Journal Options** dialog box, either the first time you use the Journal (by answering **Yes** to the message) or by **Tools - Options - Preferences** tab - **Journal Options** button.

Microsoft Outlook 2000

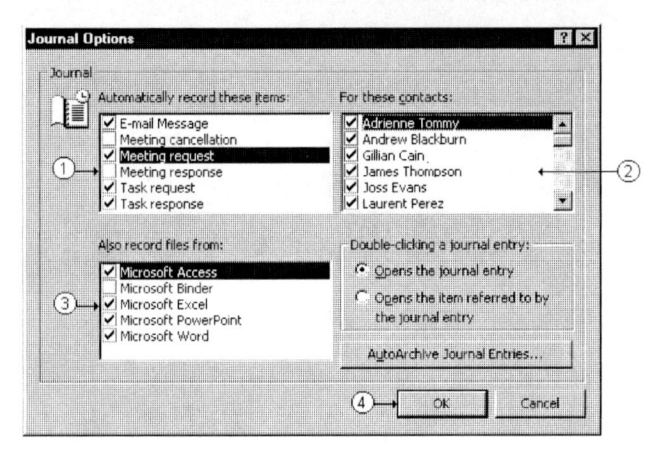

① Activate the items that Outlook must automatically record in your Journal.
② Activate the contacts for whom the specified items are to be added.
③ If you wish, you can also record the use you have made of other Office applications. The complete names of any Office documents you create or modify will appear.
④ Enter.

4.6 Favorites Folder

This folder enables you to save items, notably Web pages (or Outlook folders) that you visit regularly, making it easier to access them.

A-Going to a Web page

If necessary, display the Web toolbar (**View - Toolbars - Web**), and in the address box, enter the Web page's URL, then press Enter.

address box

⇨ You can also open a Web page by clicking a Web page shortcut that you have created in the *Outlook* bar (see 6.2 - C - Creating a shortcut to a Web page).

⇨ If you have added a Web page to the *Favorites* folder, use the *Favorites* menu to access it (see 4.6 - C - Opening a Web page from the Favorites folder).

B-Adding a Web page to the Favorites folder

▪ Go to the Web page using its shortcut or using the **Web** toolbar.
▪ **Favorites - Add to Favorites**

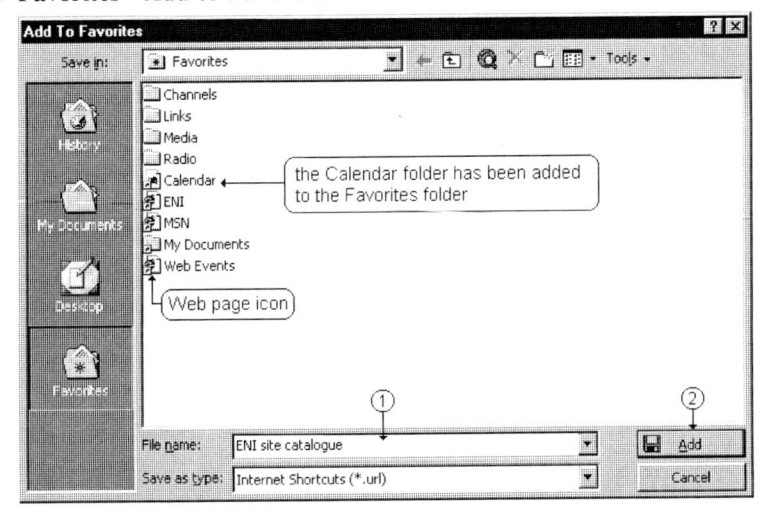

[Screenshot of the Add To Favorites dialog box, showing the Favorites folder contents: Channels, Links, Media, Radio, Calendar (with annotation "the Calendar folder has been added to the Favorites folder"), ENI, MSN, My Documents, Web Events (annotated as "Web page icon"). File name: ENI site catalogue. Save as type: Internet Shortcuts (*.url). Buttons: Add (1), Cancel (2).]

① Modify the Web page name if required.
② Click to confirm.

C-Opening a Web page from the Favorites folder

▪ Open the **Favorites** folder then click the name of the Web page you want to see.

⇨ You can also open the *Favorites* folder (by clicking its name in the *Outlook* bar or the folder list) then double clicking the Web page's name.

Microsoft Outlook 2000

5.1 Managing items

*Outlook uses the term **Item** to refer to a message, an attached document, an appointment, a task, a meeting... **Item** can refer to any element you may be working on in Outlook.*

A-Creating an item

- File - New

*The organisation of this menu list depends on which group or folder is active. For example, if you are in the **Calendar**, the first option is **Appointment**, and in **Contacts**, the first option is **Contact**.*

- Click the type of item you want to create.
- Enter its content then save the item.

⇨ *The first button on the toolbar changes according to the active group or folder. When you want to create a new item, click this button or open the list associated with it, then click on the type of item you want to create.*

B-Creating an item using a form

All Outlook items are based on forms. This said, you can choose other forms than those used by default to create contacts, messages and other items.

- File - New - Choose Form, or open the list on the New button and activate Choose Form.

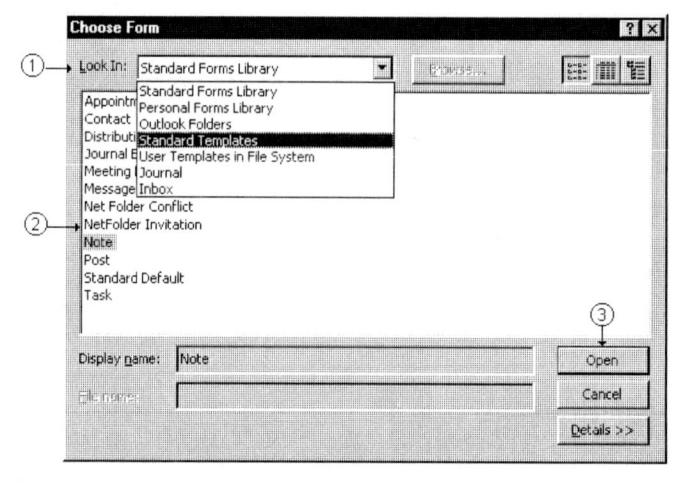

![Choose Form dialog box with callouts ①, ② and ③]

① Choose the library or the location of the form in the **Look In** list.

② Select the name of the form you want to use.

③ Confirm.
- Fill in the item's content.

C-Making an item private

By making an item private, you can hide it from the other people who access the folder.

- When you create an item, activate the **Private** option.
- Save the item.

⇨ *Calendar items that have been defined as private are preceded with a ⌧ symbol.*

D-Selecting items

- To select several adjacent items, select the first, point to the last then hold down ⇧ Shift and click.
- To select several items which are not adjacent, select the first, hold down the Ctrl key and then, without releasing it, select the other items.
- To select all the items, use the **Edit - Select All** command or Ctrl **A**.

E-Finding an item

- Activate the folder you want to search.
- **Tools**
  Find

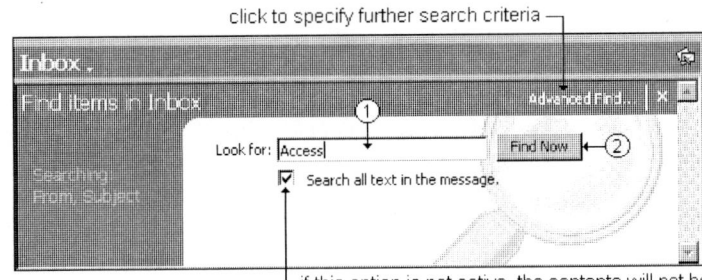

click to specify further search criteria

① Look for: Access
② Find Now

Search all text in the message.

if this option is not active, the contents will not be searched (for some items)

① Type the text to search for.
② Start searching.
- Once Outlook has finished searching, you can choose to **Go to Advanced Find** or **Clear Search**.

Microsoft Outlook 2000

F- Carrying out an advanced search

- Tools - Advanced Find or `Ctrl` `⇧ Shift` F

You can also click the **Advanced Find** button in the **Find** window.

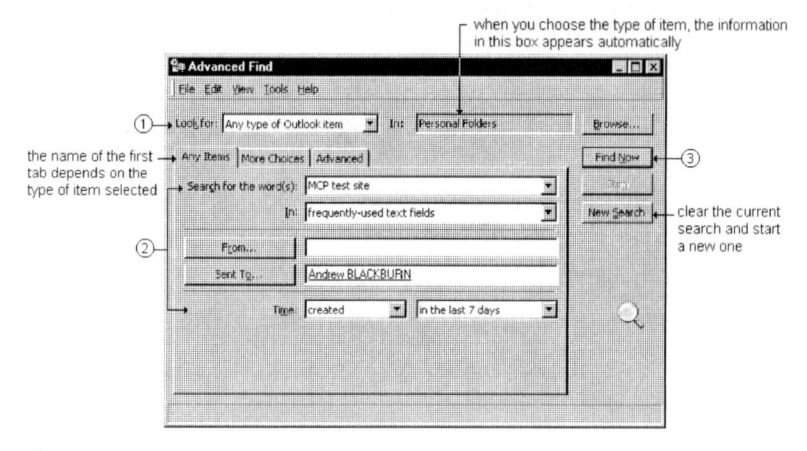

- when you choose the type of item, the information in this box appears automatically
- the name of the first tab depends on the type of item selected
- clear the current search and start a new one

① Choose what type of item you are searching for (you can look for contacts, journal entries, files, appointments, messages and so on).

② Define your search criteria.

③ Start searching.

⇨ To open one of the items, double-click it.

⇨ If the search does not find any items, **There are no items to show in this view** is shown.

⇨ To stop searching, use **File - Close** or click the ☒ button on the window.

⇨ This search feature can also be activated without starting Outlook. On the Windows desktop, open the **Start** menu, point to the **Find** option and choose **Using Microsoft Outlook**.

⇨ To save the search criteria (to make later searches easier), use **File - Save Search** and give the file a name (its extension is OSS). To use this search again, open the **Advanced Find** dialog box and open the OSS file using **File - Open Search**.

G-Moving items to another folder

- Activate the folder that contains the items you want to move then select those items.

- **Tools**
  Organize

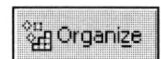

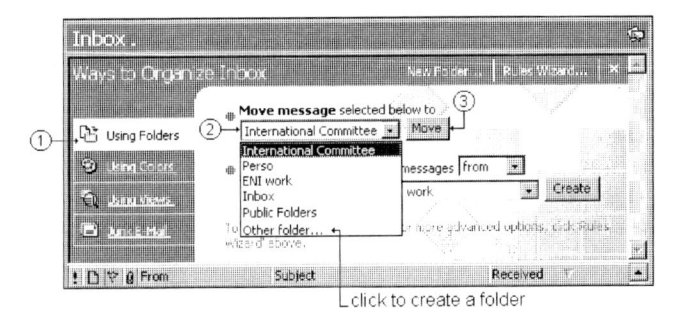

① If necessary, select this option.
② Select the destination folder.
③ Move the items.

⇨ You cannot use this technique to move items in the Calendar and Journal folders.

⇨ You can also move items by selecting them and using **Edit - Move to folder** or Ctrl ⇧Shift V, or by dragging them to the destination folder on the **Outlook** bar or in the folder list.

H-Copying items to another folder

- Activate the folder that contains the items you want to copy and select them.
- **Edit - Copy to Folder**
- Select the destination folder and click **OK**.

⇨ You can also drag the items (to the destination folder on the **Outlook** bar), holding the Ctrl key down as you drag.

I- Deleting items

This process can be carried out in two stages: the first stage transfers the deleted items into a folder which acts as a wastepaper basket, while the second stage destroys them permanently. In this way you can retrieve any items which have been deleted by mistake.

Transferring items into the Deleted Items folder

- Select the item(s) to be deleted.
- **Edit** ✗ Ctrl D
  Delete

The deleted items disappear from their original folder and are sent to the **Deleted Items** folder.

Microsoft Outlook 2000

Retrieving items deleted by mistake

- Go into the **Deleted Items** folder.
- Select the item(s) to be retrieved.
- Drag them to another folder, or use **Edit - Move to Folder** or `Ctrl` `û Shift` **V**.

Deleting items permanently

- Go into the **Deleted Items** folder.
- Select the item(s) to be permanently deleted.
- **Edit** ☒   `Ctrl` **D**
  Delete

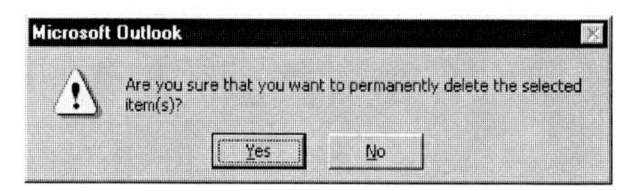

> **Microsoft Outlook**
> ⚠ Are you sure that you want to permanently delete the selected item(s)?
> [**Yes**] [No]

- Confirm with **Yes**.

➪ You can deactivate this request for confirmation by deactivating the option **Warn before permanently deleting items** in the **Advanced Options** dialog box (**Tools - Options - Other** tab - **Advanced Options** button).

➪ If you wish items to be deleted automatically when you leave Outlook, go into **Tools - Options - Other** tab, and activate the option **Empty the Deleted Items folder upon exiting**.

J- Sorting items

You can sort items whilst in **Table**, **Cards** or **Icons** view.

- **View - Current View - Customize Current View**
- Click the **Sort** button.

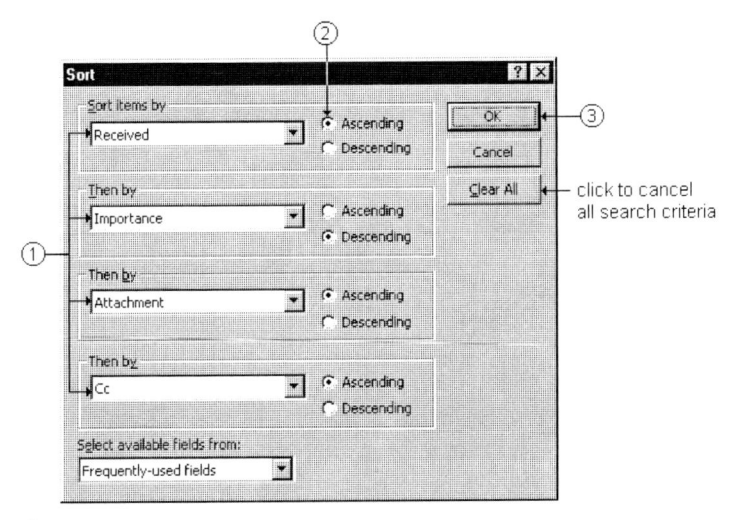

① Select the name of the field that is to be a sort criterion.
② Indicate in which order you want to sort.
③ Confirm.

⇨ *To sort a list of items in table view, click the column header you want to sort by. A black arrow to the right of the header indicates that it has been sorted. Click the header again to change the sort order. This technique is very fast, but you can only sort by one criterion at a time and you can only use the information on display.*

K-Grouping items

First method

This method is only available in Table view.

▪ If necessary, show the grouping dialog box by clicking ▭.

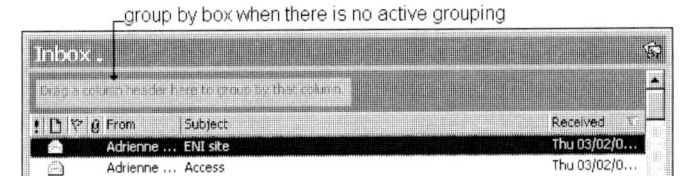

▪ Drag the header of the column by which you want to group the items onto the group by box.

Microsoft Outlook 2000

```
Inbox
From    ← the name of the group by field is shown in the group by box
! D ⛛ 0 | Subject                                          Received
  ⊞ From : Adrienne Tommy (3 items)
  ⊞ From : Andrew Blackburn (2 items)
  ⊞ From : Paul Swinson (1 item)
```
└ the lines of the table are grouped

- To expand a group, click the ⊞ button shown before the group name.
  To collapse a group, click the ⊟ sign.
- To expand/collapse all the groups, use **View - Expand/Collapse Groups**, and, depending on your requirements, click **Collapse All** or **Expand All**.

⇨ You can also right-click the name of the group field and choose to *Group By This Field*.

⇨ To remove grouping, drag the name of the field in the group by box back to the table. Be careful to insert it back into the table or it will no longer be visible.

Second method

- **View - Current View - Customize Current View**
- Click the **Group By** button.
- For each grouping criterion:

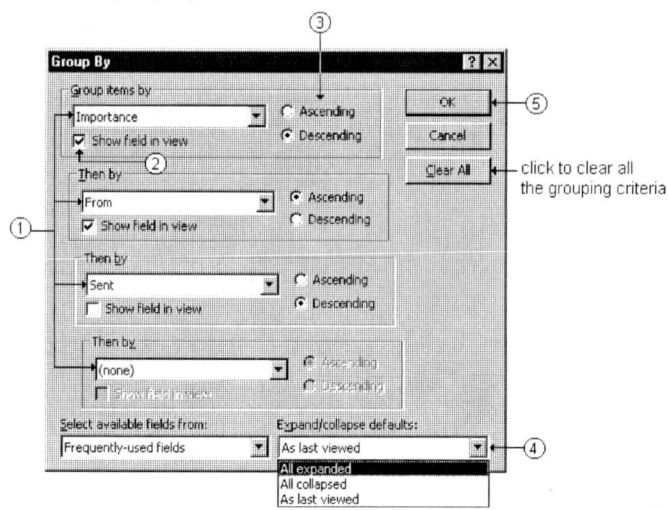

```
Group By                                          ? ×
 Group items by
  ▸│ Importance        ▼ │  ○ Ascending          OK      ←─ ⑤
     ☑ Show field in view  ● Descending       Cancel
 Then by                                        Clear All   ←─ click to clear all
  │ From              ▼ │  ● Ascending                          the grouping criteria
①─│ ☑ Show field in view  ○ Descending
 Then by
  │ Sent              ▼ │  ○ Ascending
     ☐ Show field in view  ● Descending
 Then by
  │ (none)            ▼ │  ○ Ascending
     ☐ Show field in view  ○ Descending
 Select available fields from:     Expand/collapse defaults:
 │ Frequently-used fields ▼ │    │ As last viewed     ▼ │  ←─ ④
                                  All expanded
                                  All collapsed
                                  As last viewed
```

① Select the name of the group field.
② Do you want the selected field to appear in the view.
③ Define the sort order.

④ Indicate how you want to see the groups.
⑤ Confirm.

⇨ To remove the grouping criteria, go to the **Group By** dialog box and choose the **(none)** option in the appropriate drop-down list.

L-Filtering items

Filtering items allows you to see only the data that conforms to given criteria.

- View - Current View - Customize Current View
- Click the **Filter** button.
- Define your filter criteria.

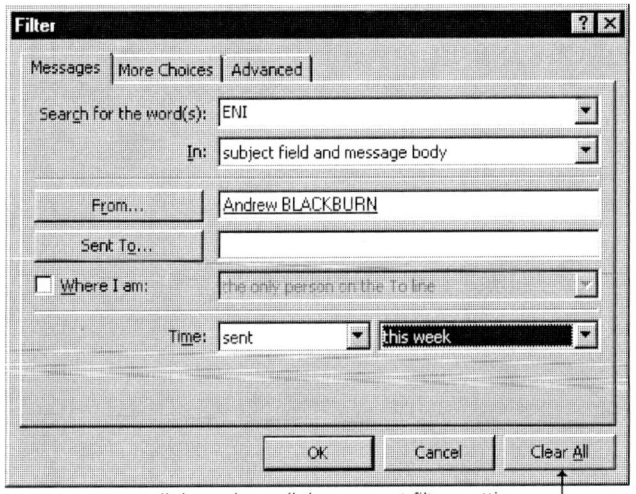

click to clear all the current filter settings

M-Printing items

- Open the folder and, if necessary, select the items to be printed.
- **File**
  Print   Ctrl P
- Choose the **Print style**.
- Start printing.

Defining the page setup before printing

- Select the item(s) concerned.
- **File - Page Setup**
- Select the print style required (these styles change according to the selected item).

Microsoft Outlook 2000   79

- On the **Format** page, define the font. Activate the option **Print using gray shading** if you want to reproduce the grey shading used in certain parts of the item (in column headings, for example).

  The Format options available depend on the item you are printing.

- On the **Paper** page define the paper format as well as its **Orientation**. Define the **Margins** to be used.

- On the **Header/Footer** page, define headers and footers, if you need them. Click in the box corresponding to the position of the text (left, centre, right) then type in the text.

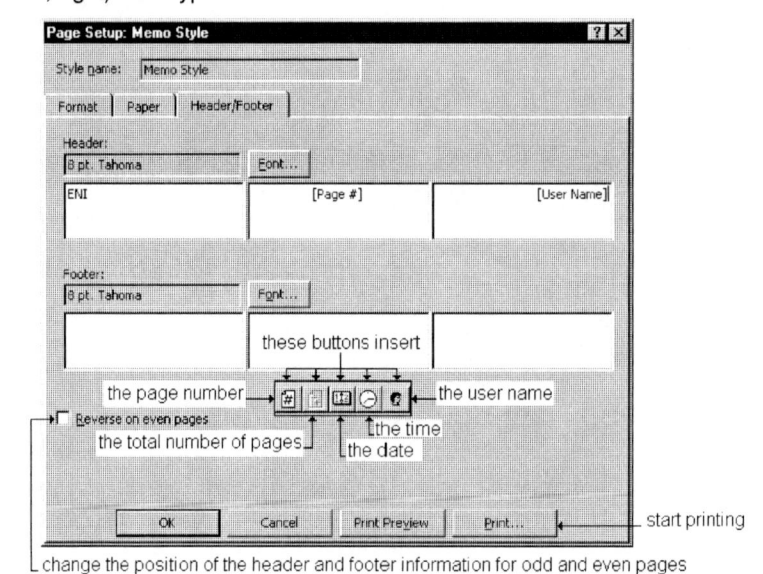

5.2 Categories of items

A-Assigning a category to an item

- While you are creating the item, click the **Categories** button.
  You can also select the item and use **Edit - Categories**.

Using an existing category

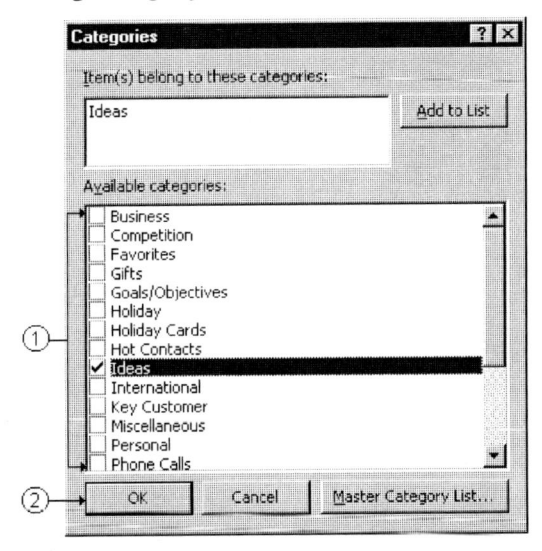

① Activate the categories which are best-suited to the item.
② Confirm.

Creating a new category

- Click the **Master Category List** button.

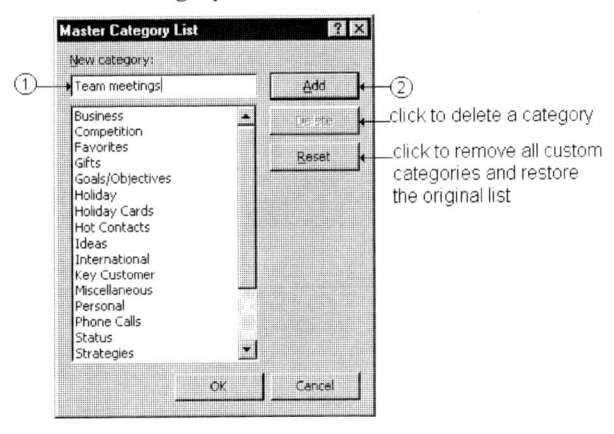

click to delete a category

click to remove all custom categories and restore the original list

Microsoft Outlook 2000

- For each new category:
  ① Enter its name.
  ② Add the new category.
- Confirm your additions by clicking **OK**.

B-Viewing items according to category

- For items other than messages, choose **View - Current View - By Category**.
- For messages, group them by **Categories** (**View - Current View - Customize Current View, Group by** button).
- Expand or collapse the categories using the [+] and [−] buttons.

C-Filtering items in a category

- **View - Current View - Customize Current View**
- Click the **Filter** button and activate the **More choices** tab.
- Click the **Categories** button and select the categories which correspond to the items you want to view.
- Click **OK** to confirm your choice of categories, then click **OK** to apply the filter.

5.3 Archiving items

A-Archiving items manually

To avoid having too many items in your Inbox you can choose to have them stored elsewhere.

- **File - Archive**

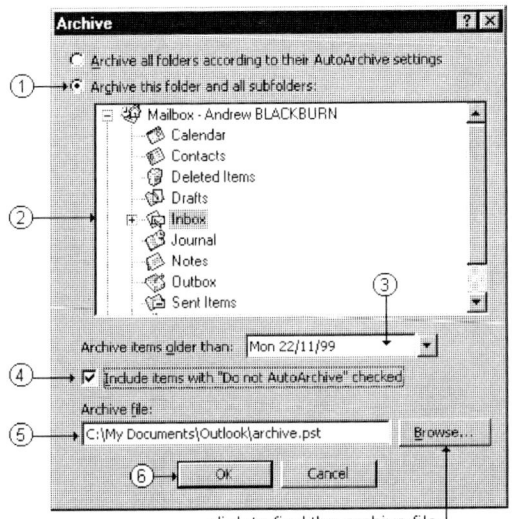

click to find the archive file

① Keep this option active.
② Select the folder to be archived.
③ Choose a cut-off date from this list.
④ Activate this option if you wish to override the **Do not AutoArchive this item** option.
⑤ Either accept the file given here or enter a new file name.
⑥ Confirm.

⇨ *Archived items disappear from their original folder.*

B-Managing items using AutoArchive

By default, every 14 days Outlook carries out an AutoArchive procedure at startup. When this happens a window appears.

Defining the rules for setting off AutoArchive at startup

- **Tools - Options - Other** tab
- Click the **AutoArchive** button.

Microsoft Outlook 2000

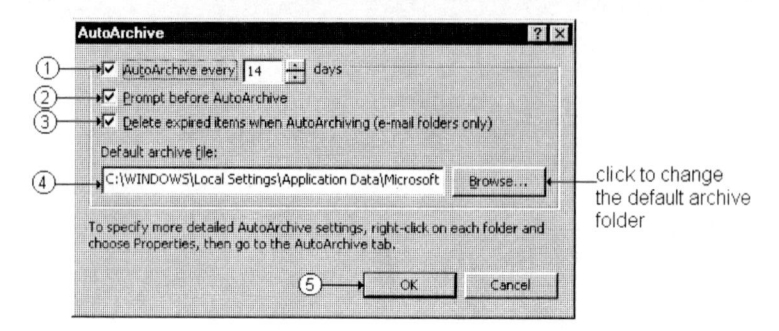

[AutoArchive dialog box with callouts ①–⑤, and note "click to change the default archive folder"]

① Define the number of days between each AutoArchive.
② Specify whether you wish to confirm each AutoArchive.
③ Indicate whether some items should be deleted at the same time as the archiving.
④ Indicate the name of the archive file.
⑤ Confirm.

⇨ *If you deactivate* **AutoArchive every***, or type 0, you will deactivate the AutoArchive at startup.*

Defining the AutoArchive rules for a folder

- Click the folder to be archived.
- **File - Folder - Properties** - **AutoArchive** tab

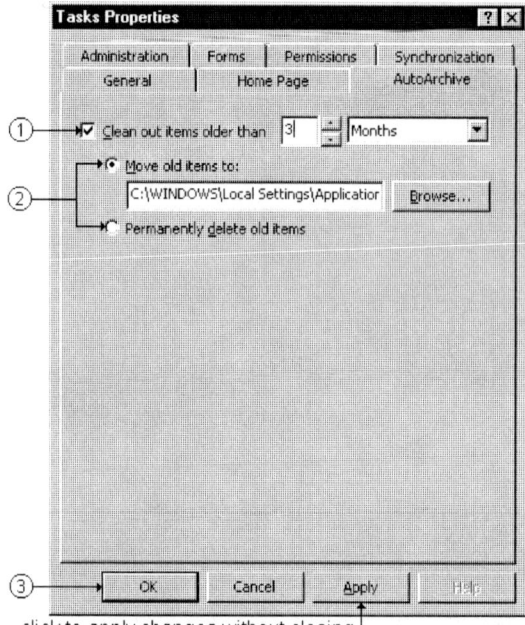

[Tasks Properties dialog with callouts ①–③]

click to apply changes without closing the dialog box

84

① Indicate the period of time after which folder items are to be auto-archived automatically.
② Indicate whether the items are to be moved into a folder (in which case specify the folder) or if they are to be deleted permanently.
③ Confirm.

Defining the AutoArchive rules for an item

- Open the item concerned.
- **File - Properties - General** tab
- Activate the **Do not AutoArchive this item** option.

6.1 Views

A-What is a view?

Views allow you to present the information contained in each folder in different ways and using different formats. The available views depend on the active folder.

- The different views can be grouped in five main types: **Table**, **Timeline**, **Cards**, **Day/Week/Month** and **Icon**.
- By default, all message folders use **Table** view, the Calendar folder is shown in **Day/Week/Month** view, the Contacts folder uses the **Cards** view, the Journal is shown as a **Timeline** and the Notes folder uses **Icons**.

⇨ *Outlook has a certain number of standard views for different folders, but you can change them and create custom views.*

B-Changing the view

- Activate the folder (any folder except Outlook Today) whose contents you want to see by clicking the folder icon.
- **View - Current View**
- Click the view you want to use.

⇨ *You can also open the **Current View** list on the **Advanced** toolbar and choose the view you want.*

⇨ *You can also click the* [Organize] *button, then click **Using views** to choose the view you want.*

C-Creating a view

- View - Current View - Define Views
- Click the **New** button.

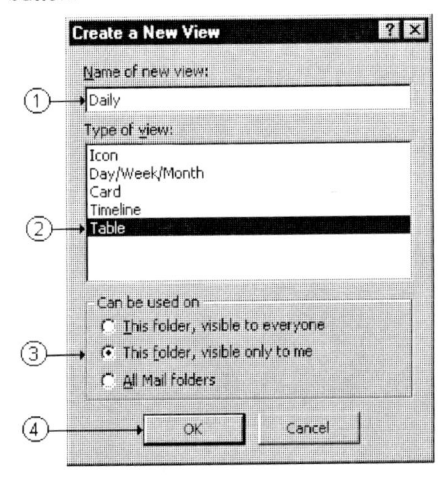

① Enter the new view's name.
② Select the type of view.
③ Define its availability.
④ Confirm.

The window that follows depends on the view you have chosen.

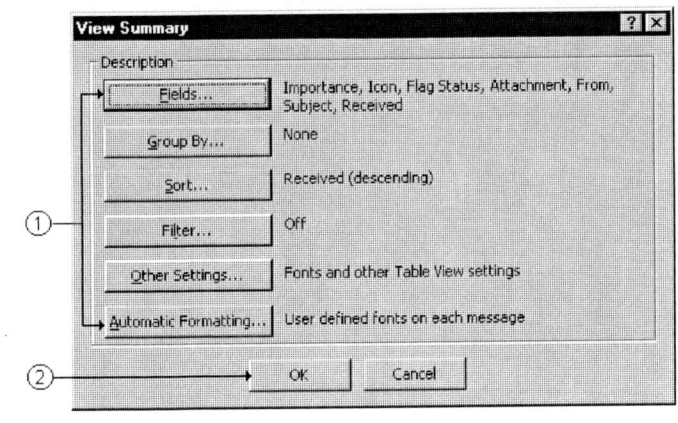

① Define the view settings.
② Confirm.

- Leave the view settings window by clicking either **Close** or **Apply View**.

Microsoft Outlook 2000

D-Managing views

▪ **View - Current View - Define Views**

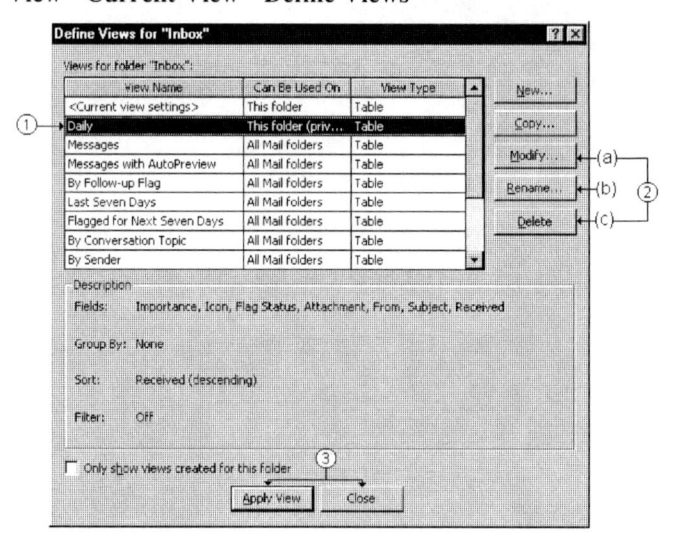

① Select the view concerned.

② Choose:

(a) to open the **View Summary** window and use the available options to make the necessary changes.

(b) to give the view a new name.

(c) to delete the selected view.

③ Leave the view definition window by clicking one of these buttons.

E-Managing view fields

*A view is defined by, amongst other things, the **fields** it contains. Each field allows you to display a specific sort of information.*

▪ **View - Current View - Customize Current View**
▪ Click the **Fields** button.

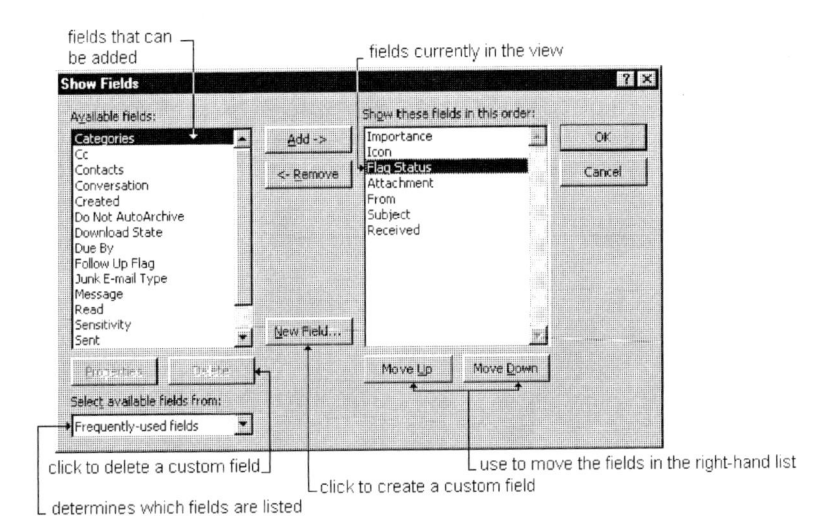

fields that can be added
fields currently in the view

[Show Fields dialog box]

click to delete a custom field
click to create a custom field
use to move the fields in the right-hand list
determines which fields are listed

Adding a field

- In the list on the right, select the field after which the new field is to be added.
- Choose the list of available fields in the **Select available fields from** drop-down list.
- In the **Available fields** list, select the field you want to see.
- Click the **Add** button.

Deleting a field

- In the right-hand list, select the field you want to remove.
- Click the **Remove** button.

⇨ *The field is deleted from the list on the right but remains in the list on the left.*

Creating a field

- Click the **New Field** button.

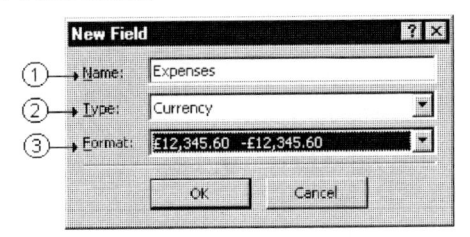

[New Field dialog box]
① Name: Expenses
② Type: Currency
③ Format: £12,345.60 -£12,345.60

① Give the new field a name.
② Choose what type of field you want to use.
③ If necessary, apply a format.

Microsoft Outlook 2000

F-Changing the width of columns

- Place the mouse pointer on the vertical line situated to the right of the header of the column you want to change.
- Drag to change the column width, or double-click to adjust the width to fit the column's contents.

G-Changing the order of columns

- Click the header of the column you want to move.
- Drag the header to the column's new position.

⇨ *Two red arrows indicate available destinations and positions that are not permitted are indicated with a big black cross.*

H-Changing the column format (Table view)

- View - Current View - Format Columns

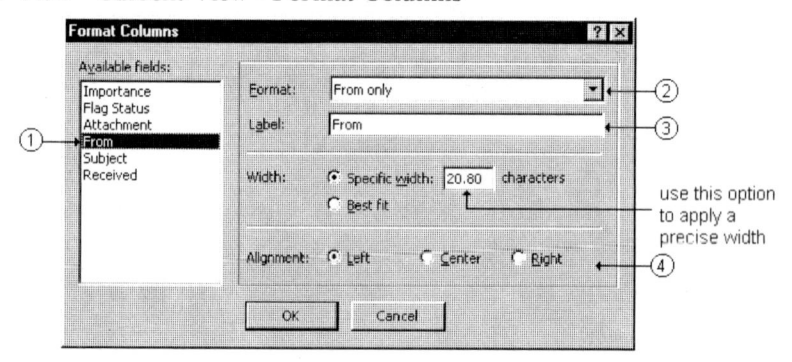

① Select the field that corresponds to the column you want to change.
② Define the view.
③ Change the column header label if you want to.
④ Choose the cell alignment and contents.

⇨ *Some column labels are fixed, which means you cannot change them.*
⇨ *To change the format of a date column, use the **Format** list.*

I- Changing the appearance of rows (Table view)

- View - Current View - Customize Current View
- Click the **Other Settings** button.

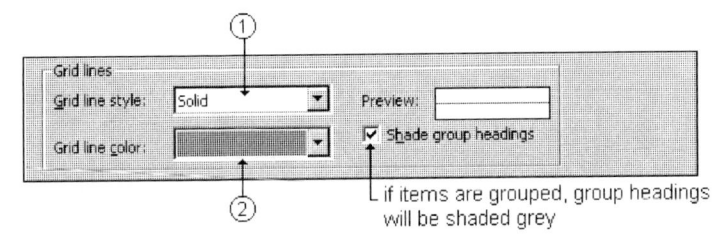

```
┌─ Grid lines ─────────────────────────────────────────┐
│   Grid line style:  [Solid        ▼]  Preview: [     ]│
│   Grid line color:  [▓▓▓▓▓▓▓▓▓▓▼]  ☑ Shade group headings│
└──────────────────────────────────────────────────────┘
```

① Open this list and choose the style of grid line.
② Choose the colour of the lines.

if items are grouped, group headings will be shaded grey

J- Showing week numbers (Timeline view)

By default, only the month and year are shown.

- View - Current View - Customize Current View
- Click the **Other Settings** button.
- Activate **Show week numbers**.

K- Showing empty fields (Cards view)

- View - Current View - Customize Current View
- Click the **Other Settings** button.
- Activate **Show empty fields**.

L- Changing the font

- View - Current View - Customize Current View
- Click the **Other Settings** button.
- For a Table view, use the **Font** button in the **Column headings** frame, the **Rows** frame or the **AutoPreview** frame to define the table characters.
- For a Timeline view, use the **Upper Scale Font**, **Lower Scale Font** and/or **Item Font** buttons.
- For Cards view, use the **Font** buttons in the **Card headings** and **Card body** frames.

Microsoft Outlook 2000

M-Authorising direct changes of data

When in-cell editing is active, you can change the contents of an item by simply clicking it (this feature is only possible in Table or Cards view).

- View - Current View - Customize Current View
- Click the **Other Settings** button.
- Activate the **Allow in-cell editing** option.

6.2 Groups and shortcuts

A-Creating a group

*A **group** consists of **shortcuts**, represented by icons, which allow the user to reach different types of folder.*

- Right-click in the **Outlook** bar and select **Add New Group**, enter the name of the group and press [Enter].

The new group is added the existing ones:

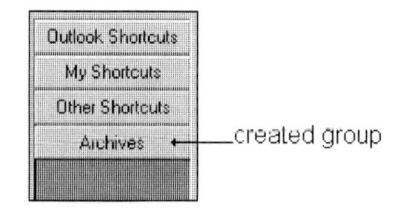

```
Outlook Shortcuts
My Shortcuts
Other Shortcuts
Archives   ←——— created group
```

- To open a group, click the button showing the group's name.
- To rename a group, right-click the group concerned, click **Rename Group**, enter the new name and press [Enter] to confirm.
- To delete a group, right-click the group concerned, click **Remove Group** and confirm the command by clicking **Yes**.

⇨ *Be careful: Outlook will delete groups even if they contain shortcuts!*

B-Creating a shortcut inside a group

▪ Open the recipient group for the shortcut.
▪ **File - New - Outlook Bar Shortcut**

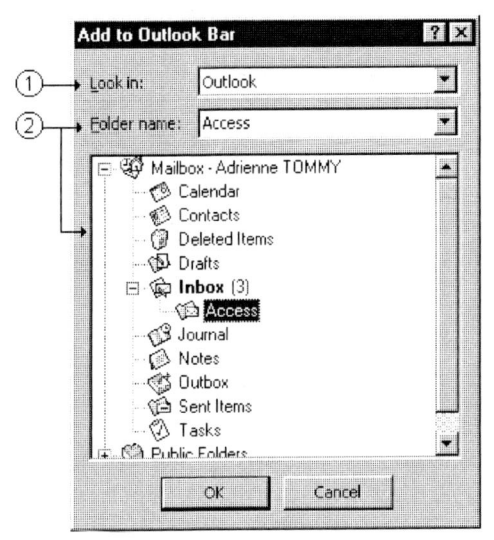

① Indicate whether it is an **Outlook** item or another folder in your **File System**.
② Select the name of the folder to be presented as a shortcut.

C-Creating a shortcut to a Web page

▪ Go to the Web page concerned.
▪ **File - New - Outlook Bar Shortcut to Web Page**
▪ Click **OK**.

Outlook tells you that the shortcut will be added to the end of the My Shortcuts group. It has the same name as the Web page.

D-Managing shortcuts

▪ To rename a shortcut, right-click the shortcut concerned, click **Rename Shortcut**, enter the new name and press [Enter] to confirm.
▪ To withdraw a shortcut, right-click the shortcut concerned, click the **Remove from Outlook Bar** option and confirm the removal by clicking **Yes**.
▪ To change the appearance of shortcut icons, right-click an empty space in the **Outlook** bar and choose **Large Icons** or **Small Icons**.

Microsoft Outlook 2000

E-Copying/moving a shortcut

- Select the shortcut to be moved or copied.
- To copy a shortcut, press [Ctrl], and, without releasing it, drag the shortcut to the position of the copy. Release the mouse button, then the [Ctrl] key.
- To move a shortcut, drag it to its new position, then release the mouse button when you are satisfied.

▷ *When you are making a copy, a plus sign (+) appears near the mouse pointer. While you are dragging the shortcut, the pointer assumes different shapes to indicate whether the move/copy is possible in that particular position.*

6.3 Folders

A-What is a folder?

- In Outlook, there are different types of folder:
  - **Outlook** or **Private Folders**: these folders contain Outlook items. You own these folders and can share them so that other users have access to them.
  - **Public Folders**: these folders enable information to be shared within a company and over the Internet using discussion groups. Public folders are created and managed by the network administrator, who also defines user permissions. These folders are only available if you are using Microsoft Exchange Server.

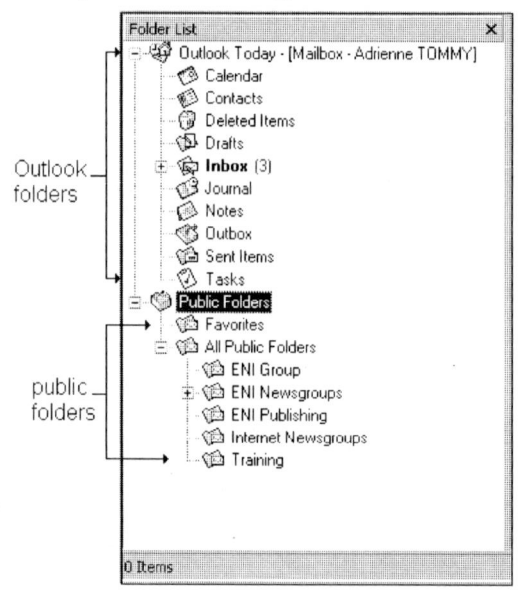

B-Creating a folder

- Open the group in which you want to make a shortcut to a new folder.
- **File - Folder - New Folder** or `Ctrl` `⇧ Shift` **E**

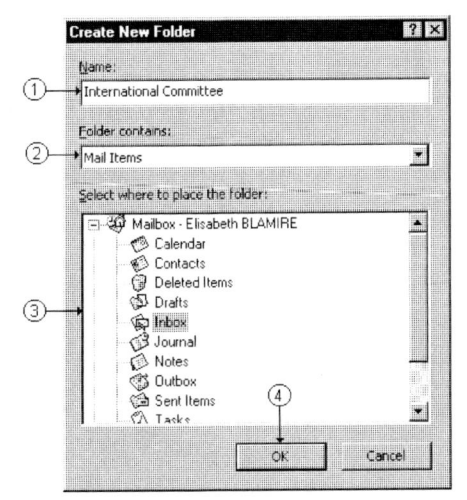

① Enter a name for the new folder.
② Indicate the type of item to be stored in the folder being created.
③ Indicate where the new folder is to be stored.
④ Confirm.

- Decide whether you want a shortcut to this folder added to the Outlook Bar.

⇨ *If you have chosen to create a shortcut on the Outlook bar, it appears in the My Shortcuts group.*

⇨ *If you have chosen to create a public folder, do not forget to define the access permissions (see 6.3 - F - Sharing folders).*

C-Managing folders

- To delete a folder, select it and use the **File - Folder - Delete** "NameOfSelectedFolder" command, then click **Yes** to confirm the deletion.
- To rename a folder, select it, use the **File - Folder - Rename** "NameOfSelectedFolder" command and enter the new name.

⇨ *These modifications only concern the folders themselves, their shortcuts are not automatically changed or deleted.*

Microsoft Outlook 2000

D-Assigning a Web page to a folder

This feature allows you to assign a Web page from the Internet or your company's intranet to a folder.

- Select the Outlook folder to which you want to assign the Web page.
- **File - Folder - Properties for**
- Click the **Home Page** tab.

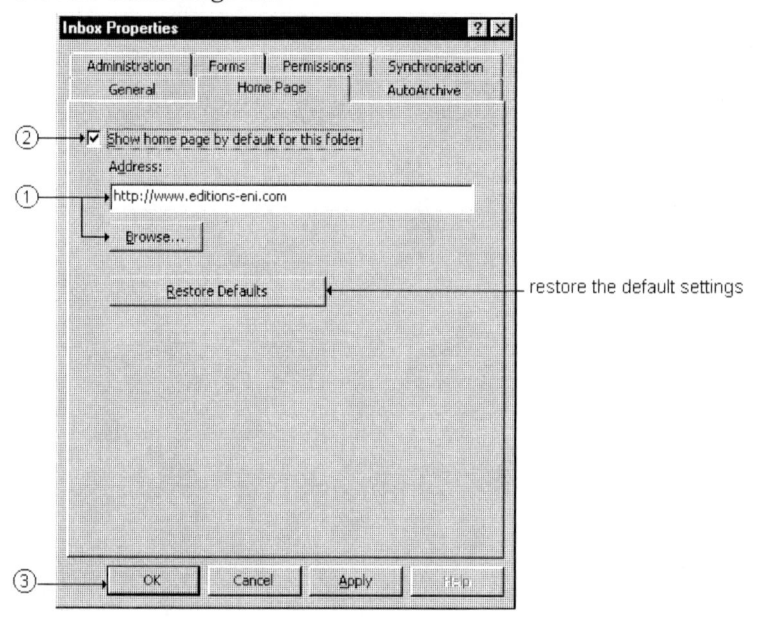

```
Inbox Properties
    Administration | Forms | Permissions | Synchronization
        General      |   Home Page    |    AutoArchive
 ②──▶ ☑ Show home page by default for this folder
      Address:
 ①──▶ http://www.editions-eni.com
      Browse...
              Restore Defaults  ◀────── restore the default settings


 ③──▶    OK        Cancel      Apply       Help
```

① Enter the URL address of the Web page you want to display (you can use the **Browse** button to select the address).
② Activate this option if you want the Web page to appear when you click the folder's name.
③ Confirm.

⇨ *When the Show home page by default for this folder option is active, clicking the folder name will display the home page, and a second click will open the folder. If this option is not active, you can display the home page usign View - Show Folder Home Page.*

E-Using a public folder

To use this feature you must have permission to read, create and modify the items in the public folder (see. 6.3 - F - Sharing folders).

- Open, if necessary, the folder list (**View - Folder list**).
- Expand the **Public Folders** list by clicking the + sign that appears before the name.
- Click the name of the folder you want to use.

- File - New - Post in This Folder or [Ctrl][⇧ Shift] S
- Complete the item as appropriate.
- Click the [Post] button.

F- Sharing folders

This feature is only available if you are working with Microsoft Exchange Server.
By using this feature you can assign permission to access, change, create or delete items in your folder(s). You may only do this if you are the owner of the folder.

- Select the folder.
- **File - Folder - Properties for "NameOfSelectedFolder"**
- Activate the **Permissions** tab.

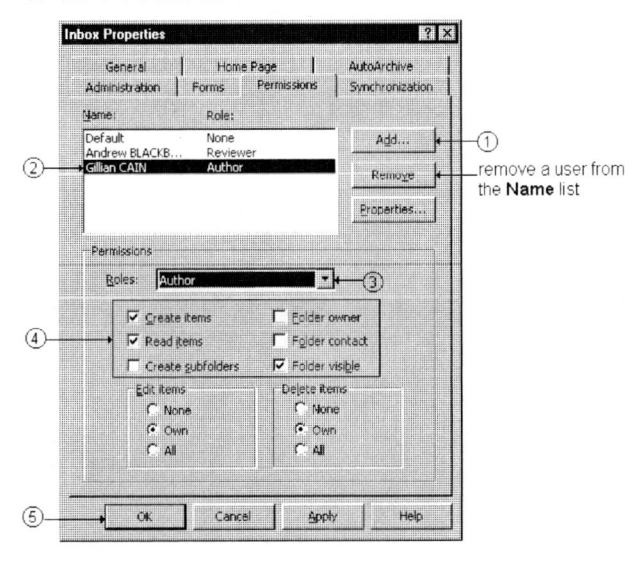

① Select all the users to whom you wish to give permissions. Click **OK** to confirm.
② Select the user whose access permissions you want to define.
③ Select the permission level to be assigned:

Owner	Maximum permissions.
Publishing Editor	Permission to create, read, modify and delete all items and files, and create sub-folders.
Editor	Permission to create, read, modify and delete all items and files.
Publishing Author	Permission to create and read items and files, modify and delete any files which you may have created, and create subfolders.

Microsoft Outlook 2000

Author	Permission to create and read items and files, and to change and delete files you have created.
Non-editing Author	Permission to create and read items and files.
Reviewer	Permission only to read items and files.
Contributor	Permission only to create items and files. The folder contents are not revealed.
None	No permission to open the folder.

④ Use these options to redefine the selected permission.

⑤ Confirm.

⇨ To check your permissions levels, open the folder list and right-click the folder concerned. Choose the **Properties** option then click the **Summary** page. Your permission level is shown under **Permissions**. If the **Permissions** page replaces the **Summary** page it is because you have owner permissions. If neither of these pages is available, you do not have permissions for the selected folder.

G-Opening another user's folder

- File - Open - Other User's Folder
- In the **Name** box, enter the e-mail address to be used.
- Open the **Folder** list and select the one you want to open.
- Click **OK**.

If you do not have permission to open the folder, Outlook displays this message:

[Microsoft Outlook dialog: Unable to display the folder. The Inbox folder could not be found.]

Otherwise the folder is open. Note that you cannot change this folder.

⇨ To leave another user's folder, use the **File - Exit** command, or click the ⊠ button in the window.

MENU SHORTCUT KEYS

File
  New
    Post in this folder   `Ctrl` `Shift` **S**
    Folder   `Ctrl` `Shift` **E**
    Appointment   `Ctrl` `Shift` **A**
    Meeting request   `Ctrl` `Shift` **Q**
    Contact   `Ctrl` `Shift` **C**
    Distribution list   `Ctrl` `Shift` **L**
    Task   `Ctrl` `Shift` **K**
    Task request   `Ctrl` `Shift` **U**
    Journal entry   `Ctrl` `Shift` **J**
    Note   `Ctrl` `Shift` **N**
    Office document   `Ctrl` `Shift` **H**
  Open
    Selected items   `Ctrl` **O**
  Folder
    New folder   `Ctrl` `Shift` **E**
  Print   `Ctrl` **P**
  Exit   `Alt` `F4`

Edit
  Undo   `Ctrl` **Z**
  Cut   `Ctrl` **X**
  Copy   `Ctrl` **C**
  Paste   `Ctrl` **V**
  Clear   `Del`
  Select all   `Ctrl` **A**
  Delete   `Ctrl` **D**
  Move to folder   `Ctrl` `Shift` **V**
  Mark as read   `Ctrl` **Q**

View
  Go to
    Folder   `Ctrl` **Y**
    Inbox   `Ctrl` `Shift` **I**

Microsoft Outlook 2000

Tools

Synchronise
    All folders — `F9`
Address book — `Ctrl` `⇧ Shift` **B**
Advanced Find — `Ctrl` `⇧ Shift` **F**

Macro

Macros — `Alt` `F8`
Visual Basic Editor — `Alt` `F11`

Actions

New "item" — `Ctrl` **N**
Forward — `Ctrl` **F**
Reply — `Ctrl` **R** (Inbox folder)
Reply to all — `Ctrl` `⇧ Shift` **R** (Inbox folder)
New meeting request — `Ctrl` `⇧ Shift` **Q** (Calendar folder)
New distribution list — `Ctrl` `⇧ Shift` **L** (Contacts folder)
Flag for follow up — `Ctrl` `⇧ Shift` **G** (Contacts folder)
New task request — `Ctrl` `⇧ Shift` **U** (Tasks folder)

Help

Microsoft Outlook Help — `F1`
What's This? — `⇧ Shift` `F1`

OTHER SHORTCUT KEYS

Calendar

Show 2 days through 9 days — `Alt` key for number of days
Show 10 days — `Alt` **0**
Show weeks — `Alt` **-**
Show months — `Alt` **=**
In month view:
    Go to the first day — `Alt` `Pg Up`
    Go to the last day — `Alt` `Pg Dn`

COMMON TOOLS

*Outlook has three toolbars: the **Standard** toolbar, the **Advanced** toolbar and the **Web** toolbar. The **Standard** and **Advanced** toolbars contain tools particular to each folder, and the **Web** toolbar contains tools common to all folders.*

Tools on the Standard toolbar common to all folders

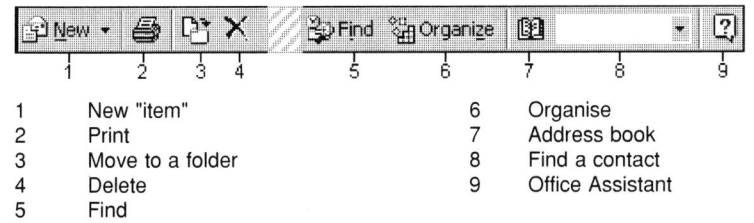

1	New "item"	6	Organise
2	Print	7	Address book
3	Move to a folder	8	Find a contact
4	Delete	9	Office Assistant
5	Find		

Tools on the Advanced toolbar common to all folders

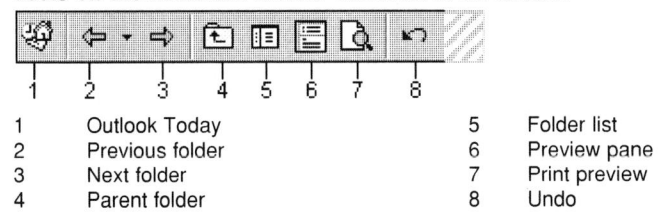

1	Outlook Today	5	Folder list
2	Previous folder	6	Preview pane
3	Next folder	7	Print preview
4	Parent folder	8	Undo

Web toolbar (common to all folders)

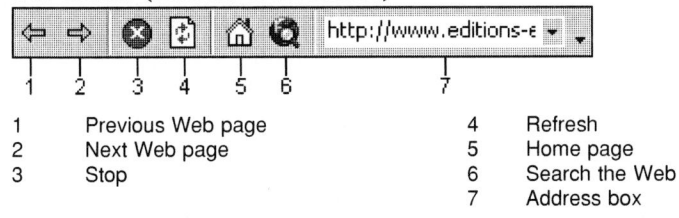

1	Previous Web page	4	Refresh
2	Next Web page	5	Home page
3	Stop	6	Search the Web
		7	Address box

TOOLBARS FOR THE MAIN FOLDERS

Inbox

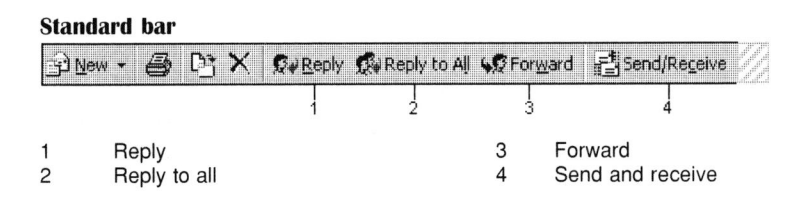

Standard bar

1	Reply	3	Forward
2	Reply to all	4	Send and receive

Microsoft Outlook 2000

Advanced bar

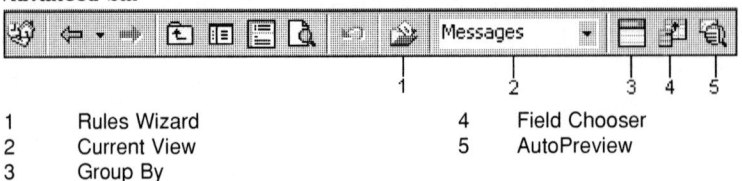

1	Rules Wizard	4	Field Chooser
2	Current View	5	AutoPreview
3	Group By		

Calendar Folder

Standard bar

1	Go to today	4	Week
2	Day	5	Month
3	Work Week		

Advanced bar

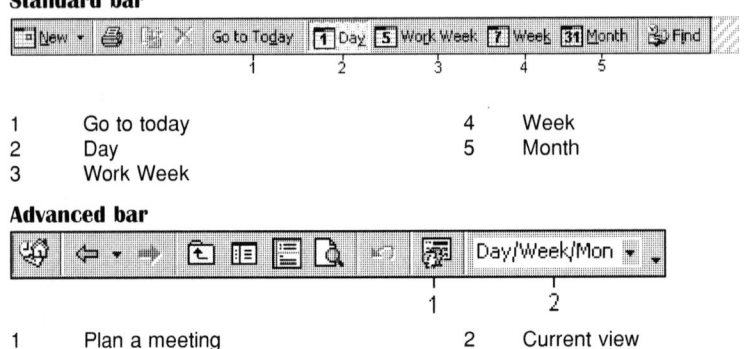

1	Plan a meeting	2	Current view

Contacts Folder

Standard bar

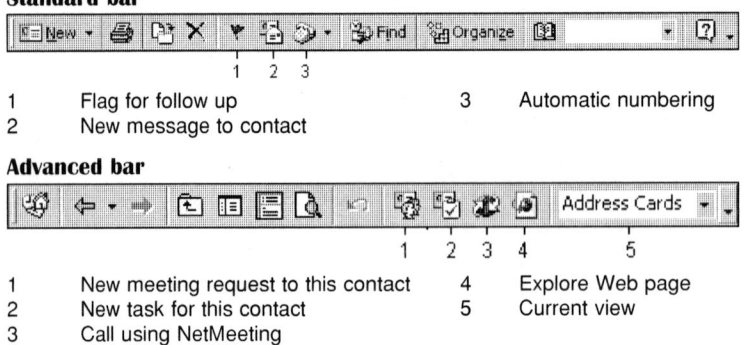

1	Flag for follow up	3	Automatic numbering
2	New message to contact		

Advanced bar

1	New meeting request to this contact	4	Explore Web page
2	New task for this contact	5	Current view
3	Call using NetMeeting		

Tasks folder

Standard bar
The *Standard* toolbar is identical to the common bar.

Advanced bar

1	Current view	3	Field Chooser
2	Group by box	4	AutoPreview

Notes Folder

Standard bar

1	Large icons	3	List
2	Small icons		

Advanced bar

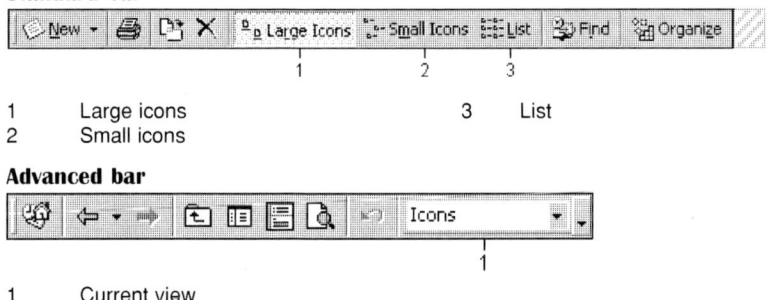

1   Current view

Journal folder

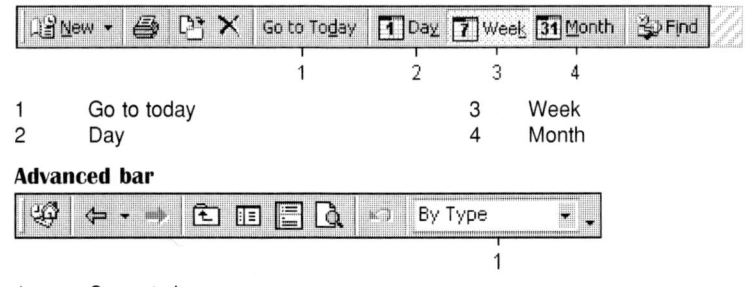

Standard bar

1	Go to today	3	Week
2	Day	4	Month

Advanced bar

1   Current view

Microsoft Outlook 2000

Inbox Folder

High/Low priority message	
Read/unread message	
Forwarded Message	
Message that has been replied to	
Saved or unsent message	
Coded message	
Message with digital ID	
Message noted incorrect	
Microsoft Mail 3.x form	
Meeting request	
Accepted/tentatively accepted/refused request	
Cancelled meeting	
Task request	
Accepted/refused task request	
Message with an attachment	
Message flagged for follow-up	
Message marked as complete	

Calendar Folder

Appointment

Meeting

Meeting request

Recurring appointment

Recurring appointment or meeting

Appointment or meeting reminder

Private appointment or meeting

Start and end times of appointment or meeting

Calendar item with attachment

Activities for this contact saved in Journal automatically

Contacts Folder

Contact

Contact with attachment

104

Contact flagged for follow up

Contact marked as completed

Distribution list

Tasks Folder

Task

Accepted/refused task

Finished tasks

Task assigned to another person/to you

Task with an attachment

High/low priority task

Task in progress

Recurring task

Journal Folder

Appointment

Appointment request, appointment reply, meeting, meeting request, meeting replies

Cancelled meeting

Conversation

Document

E-Mail message

Fax

Letter

Microsoft Access Database

Microsoft Excel Workbook

Microsoft PowerPoint Presentation

Microsoft Word Document

Note

Phone call

Task

Task request/task request reply

Remote Session

Journal item with an attachment

Microsoft Outlook 2000

A

ABSENCE

Managing messages during your absence — 27

ADDRESS BOOKS

Description — 60

ADDRESSEES

See RECIPIENTS

ALARM

Setting (Calendar) — 40

APPOINTMENTS

Creating (Calendar) — 36
See also CALENDAR

ARCHIVING

Defining a folder's AutoArchive rules — 84
Defining an item's AutoArchive rules — 85
Defining the AutoArchive rules for a folder — 84
Items automatically (AutoArchive) — 83
Items manually — 82

ASSISTANT

Out of Office Assistant — 27

ATTACHMENTS

Attaching a document — 20

AVAILABILITY

Defining (Calendar) — 41

C

CALENDAR

Changing Date Navigator view — 49
Changing the date — 35
Creating a meeting — 42
Creating an appointment — 36
Creating an event — 37
Defining working week/hours — 49
Defining your availability — 41
Managing items — 38
Previewing — 48
Printing — 47
Printing items — 48
Repeating items — 39
Saving as a Web page — 35
Selecting contacts before creating a meeting — 43
Setting a reminder alarm — 40
Viewing — 32
Viewing a month — 33
Viewing a week — 34
See also MEETINGS

CATEGORIES

Assigning a category to an item — 81
Creating — 81

COLOUR

Applying to messages from a particular contact — 29
Applying background colour to a message — 23

COLUMNS

Changing the format (Table view) — 90
Changing the order (View) — 90
Changing the width (View) — 90

CONTACTS

Address books — 60
Calling — 54
Creating — 52
Creating a distribution list — 58
Flagging — 56
Going to the Contacts folder — 52
Managing links — 56
Printing — 57
Selecting before creating a meeting — 43

COPYING

Items to another folder — 75
Shortcuts — 94

D

DELETING

Items — 75
Retrieving items deleted by mistake — 76

DISTRIBUTION LIST

New	58

E

ENVIRONMENT

Description	2

EVENTS

Creating (Calendar)	37
See also CALENDAR	

F

FAVORITES

Adding a Web page	71
Using the Favorites Folder	70

FILTERING

Items	79
Items in a category	82

FINDING

Carrying out an advanced search	74
Items	73

FOLDER LIST

Description	4

FOLDERS

Assigning a Web page	96
Calendar	32
Contacts	52
Creating	95
Defining AutoArchive rules	84
Description	94
Favorites Folder	70
Journal folder	68
Managing	95
Notes folder	65
Opening another user's folder	98
Sharing	97
Tasks	60
Using a public folder	96

FOLLOWING UP

Contacts	56
Messages	11

FORMATTING

Default message format	25
HTML messages	23
Message text	19
Paragraphs	19

FORMS

Creating an item using a form	72

FORWARDING

Messages	16
Notes	66

G

GROUPING

Items	77

GROUPS

Creating	92
Creating a shortcut inside a group	93
Managing	92

H

HIDING

Preview pane	5

HTML

Formatting HTML messages	23

HYPERLINK

Inserting	24

I

IMPORTANCE

Of a message	12

Microsoft Outlook 2000

INSERTING

Attachments	20
Horizontal line	23
Hyperlink	24
Objects	22
Outlook item	21
Pictures	23
Signatures	20

INTERNET/INTRANET

Creating an online meeting	46

ITEMS

Archiving	82
Assigning a category to an item	81
Copying to another folder	75
Creating	72
Creating with a form	72
Defining the AutoArchive rules	85
Deleting	75
Filtering	79
Finding	73
Grouping	77
Inserting	21
Making an item private	73
Managing	72
Managing Calendar items	38
Moving to another folder	74
Printing	79
Printing Calendar items	48
Repeating (Calendar)	39
Selecting	73
Sorting	76

J

JOURNAL

Creating an entry manually	69
Creating automatic entries	69
Opening	68

L

LEAVING

Microsoft Outlook	1

M

MEETINGS

Adding/withdrawing a request to attend	45
Cancelling	45
Creating	42
Online meeting	46
Replying to a meeting request	44
Viewing the replies to a meeting request	45

See also CALENDAR

MENUS

Using	1

MESSAGE OPTIONS

Defining delivery options	14
Defining the nature	12
Importance rating	12
Requesting a delivery receipt	13
Requesting a read receipt	13
Sending messages with tracking options	13

MESSAGES

Asking to be notified when a new message arrives	27
Creating	6
Creating with stationery	7
Default message format	25
Flagging	11
Formatting	19
Formatting an HTML message	23
Forwarding	16
Managing during your absence	27
Managing unwanted mail	30
Managing with the Rules Wizard	30
Marking as read or unread	15
Organising	29
Printing	24
Reading a message you have received	14
Recalling/replacing	10
Replying to	15
Saving and closing an unfinished message	8
Sending	9
Sending a message again	10
Whose reply involves voting	13

See also MESSAGE OPTIONS

MICROSOFT OUTLOOK

Starting/leaving 1
Workspace 2

MOVING

Items to another folder 74
Messages from a particular contact 29
Shortcuts 94

N

NEW

Category 81
Contact 52
Folder 95
Group 92
Item 72
Message 6
Note 66
View 87

NOTES

Changing the characteristics 66
Changing the icons view 67
Changing the size of the window 67
Creating 66
Forwarding 66
Reading/editing 66
The Notes folder 65

NUISANCE

Managing unwanted mail 30

O

OBJECTS

Inserting 22

OPENING

Another user's folder 98

ORGANISING

Folders 74
Messages from a particular contact 29

OUTLOOK BAR

Description 2

OUTLOOK ITEMS

See ITEMS

OUTLOOK TODAY

Customising 51
Description 50

P

PARAGRAPHS

Formatting 19

PICTURES

Inserting 23
Inserting a background picture 23

PREVIEW PANE

Showing/hiding 5

PRINT PREVIEW

Viewing the Calendar 48

PRINTING

Calendar 47
Calendar items 48
Contacts 57
Items 79
Messages 24

R

RECALLING

Messages 10

RECEIPTS

Requesting 13

RECIPIENTS

Selecting before creating a message 10

REMINDER

See ALARM, CALENDAR

Microsoft Outlook 2000

REPLACING

Messages ... 10

REPLYING

To a meeting request ... 44
To a message ... 15
To a task request ... 63
Voting in reply to a message ... 18

ROWS

Changing the appearance
(Table view) ... 91

RULES WIZARD

Using to manage messages ... 30

S

SAVING

An unfinished message ... 8
Calendar as a Web page ... 35

SCREEN

Description ... 2

SELECTING

Contacts for a meeting ... 43
Items ... 73

SENDING

A message twice ... 10
A voting message ... 13
A Web page in a message ... 8
Messages ... 9
Messages with tracking options ... 13

SHARING

Folders ... 97

SHORTCUTS

Copying/moving ... 94
Creating inside a group ... 93
Managing ... 93
To a Web page ... 93

SHOWING

Preview pane ... 5

SIGNATURES

Creating ... 26
Inserting into a message ... 20

SORTING

Items ... 76

SPELLING

Checking the spelling in a message ... 18

STARTING

Microsoft Outlook ... 1

T

TASKS

Assigning a task to somebody else ... 62
Creating a recurring task ... 63
Defining tracking options ... 65
Replying to a task request ... 63
Reporting on a task's progress ... 64
Setting yourself a task ... 61

TELEPHONE CALLS

Calling a contact ... 54
Creating a Speed Dial list ... 55

TEXT

Formatting ... 19

V

VIEW

Authorising direct changes of data ... 92
Calendar views ... 32
Changing ... 86
Changing Date Navigator view ... 49
Changing the appearance of rows
(Table view) ... 91
Changing the column format
(Table view) ... 90
Changing the font ... 91
Changing the Icons view
(Notes folder) ... 67
Changing the order of columns ... 90
Changing the width of columns ... 90
Creating ... 87

Description	86
Items by category	82
Managing	88
Managing view fields	88
Outlook Today	50
Showing empty fields (Cards view)	91
Showing week numbers (Timeline view)	91
Showing/hiding the preview pane	5

VOTING

| In reply to a message | 18 |

W

WEB PAGE

Adding to the Favorites folder	71
Assigning to a folder	96
Creating a shortcut to a Web page	93
Opening from the Favorites folder	71
Saving the Calendar as a Web page	35
Sending in a message	8

Microsoft Outlook 2000